KAUA'I KIDS In Peace And War

CHILDHOOD ON A REMOTE ISLAND

AND WORLD WAR TWO

by

Bill Fernandez

Printed in the United States of America

All photographs used with permission from Kaua'i Historical Society except Cane Fire which is used with the generous permission of photographer Brian Howell of Kaua'i.

Library of Congress LLCN 2012917960

1. Fernandez , Bill – Childhood and youth. 2. Fernandez, Judith – Photographer. 3. Kapa'a, Kaua'i Biography. 4. Native Hawaiian customs and practices. 5. Social life and customs – 20th century. 6. Sugar plantations – Kaua'i. 7. Pearl Harbor – World War II – military occupation Hawai'i – Japanese internment – go-fers – Ni'ihau

ISBN-13 978-1479384914

ISBN-10 1479384917

1. Hawai'i Non-fiction 2. Memoir – childhood
Published by Makani Kai Media
www.kauaibillfernandez.com   facebook: Bill Fernandez Hawaiian Author

Publishers Weekly Review:

"In this candid memoir, Hawaii native Fernandez (Rainbows over Kapa'a) describes his hometown and the effects of the war on his childhood on the ethnically diverse island of Kaua'i. The narrative, which weaves childhood adventures with historical references, begins in peacetime with Fernandez growing up blissfully unaware of global troubles outside of his island. On an island laden with natural beauty, people trust ancient beliefs in kahunas, spiritual experts with "magical powers that can shrivel your body or snatch your soul." ... surrounded by more than 20 ethnic groups, Fernandez explains "the Hawaiian way" of sharing "what you had with friends or strangers,"... Colorful recollections of learning how to swim, searching for ...flying Santa Claus, learning about life while polishing shoes for American soldiers, and his parents' investment in a New York–style theater... [He] depicts wartime changes ...after the attack on Pearl Harbor: conflicts and tension between residents and their Japanese neighbors who feared internment; and the effect of soldiers in town... this is an honest retelling of one native's experience during the war...of particular interest to those interested in Hawaiian history. " Reviewed on: 04/22/2013

Contents

Part One – Peace

Part Two – War

Dedication

This book is dedicated to my childhood friends
Sooky and Renee Fernandes
and
to my wife Judith, without her efforts these stories
would not have been published

Preface

I began my life in isolation. The world that I knew was a small island surrounded by ocean. Nothing else existed, for there were no radios, TV, or internet. Growing up on Kaua'i, children had nothing. You made what you needed to amuse yourself.

My homeland was populated by more than twenty different ethnic groups, many of whom did not speak English. The only common language was Pidgin, a bastardization of several different dialects. This meant that communication was limited and knowledge of the world outside of my island miniscule.

Despite this ethnic diversity, there was no warfare among the races. This was true even though the vast majority of us lived in a state of poverty. Why did we get along? Because it is the Hawaiian way to share and help each other without expectation of reward. Although it was a struggle to survive, this communal spirit made growing up on Kaua'i the best of times.

My story concentrates, in its first half, on living a life of indolence on a remote island. The sudden realization that you must educate yourself and care about tomorrow came with the Japanese attack on Pearl Harbor. The second half describes the problems brought on by war. On December 7th, 1941, the population of Kaua'i was forty-two percent Japanese. More troublesome was the landing on Ni'ihau of an enemy pilot. Aided by two Japanese citizens of America he terrorized the island until his death.

On our island, twenty miles from Ni'ihau, we wondered: what would happen if we were invaded? There were just a few National Guardsmen to defend us. One-half of them were Japanese. My story portrays the fears and uncertainties of those dark months at the start of the war. Declaration of martial law sent the authorities into an insane frenzy. Friends and family members felt the threat of internment. You will learn of the struggle of

American citizens to escape imprisonment and prove their loyalty to our country. Military authority dictated to us, disregarding rights and imposing draconian rules. The common people and kids tried to cope with being on a wartime frontline and the news of American defeats in battle.

War may be the ultimate human insanity, but it can change lives for the better. Come with me as I tell my story of childhood indolence and my transition into a thirst for knowledge to better my life and the lives of others.

Aloha nui loa, Bill Fernandez 2013

Part One

PEACE

CHAPTER 1

Games

Mahapi means, "I'll do it tomorrow." It's a word you will not find in any dictionary. It may be pidgin English for "Me Happy." Those I grew up with used the word to describe our belief that doing something today was not important. We lived trapped on a speck of land, surrounded by an ocean with nowhere to go. Kaua'i is a huge rock drenched in sunshine, cooled by gentle breezes, and perfumed by flowers.

I'm sure you will say that I was lazy for postponing what could be done today for tomorrow. But consider this: on my island you lived in an atmosphere where the troubles of the world did not exist. Without radios, telegraph, or newspapers, I did not know that Adolf Hitler had denounced the Treaty of Versailles and re-armed Germany. I did not realize that Japan threatened war with China. Nor did I understand President Roosevelt's New Deal promoting unionism and collective bargaining.

All of these distant events would change our lives. But in my early years, we lived without outside stresses. We lived in an atmosphere that was like a pleasant drug which induced a hypnosis dulling the senses.

None of us had money. You made everything you wanted. The few steamers that came to the island brought goods for the plantations and pineapple canneries. They didn't have cargo space to bring toys for kids.

I grew up in Waipouli, a suburb of Kapa'a. Although many races had been imported to work the sugar fields, Waipouli contained only three: Japanese, Portuguese, and Hawaiians. As might be expected, alliances formed along racial lines. I was in the peculiar position of being a member of both the Portuguese gang and the Hawaiian gang.

What did this mean? It meant competition, warfare, espionage, and the search for technological supremacy. Playing Cowboys and Indians did not have much excitement when you aimed a pointed finger at an opponent and said, "Bang, you're dead." But when Hogan, the leader of the Japanese boys, gathered a sheaf of cane tassels, inserted a nail on one end, feathered the other end, and fired a missile with a hau wood bow, you knew you were out of the game when you got hit.

"No fair," I yelled at Hogan. But he just gave me a deadpan look. To counter this breaking of the finger-gun rules, the Portuguese gang came up with an ancient weapon, the slingshot. Find a Y-shaped tree branch. Strip it. Notch the ends. Acquire a castaway inner tube at the neighborhood garage. Cut strips of rubber and attach them to the V-shaped ends of the branch. Add a leather pouch and, *voila,* a missile weapon. Flinging small pine cone seeds with your slingshot, you knew you had struck an enemy when he howled from the sting of impact. But mind you, pine cones do not do lasting damage like a cane tassel arrow.

Things got out of hand in our warfare when someone decided to reverse the nail in the arrow. Instead of being hit by the blunt end of the metal, you were pricked by the pointed end. Retaliation followed as the slingshot ammo switched from pine cones to stones. The howling really ramped up when your opponent got walloped with a rock. All this lethality came to a sudden stop when an injured Indian complained to his parents.

What a sore loser. The cowboys suffered severe spankings, administered by a lathe stick swatted across bare legs. This punishment left red welts that hurt for hours. Parents confiscated slingshots and arrows. The gangs had to find some other way to compete.

Despite the corporal punishment that ended the game of "Cowboys and Indians," the credo of "I'm superior to you" smoldered unabated. There weren't organized sports to participate in. So what could kids do?

My friend Raymond came up with an idea. "Look at this," he said, showing me a picture. "Hawaiians are riding the waves at Waikiki."

It puzzled me. Riding the waves just wasn't done in Kapa'a. The missionaries had banned surf riding as "an idle pleasure." They said, "The time spent on surfing could be better spent working."

At the same time Raymond came up with his novel idea, Hogan and his gang did the prohibited act. I saw the Japanese riding waves at Waipouli Beach and thought that God would strike them down. But He didn't. I was astounded that they got away with their sacrilege.

Jealously, I watched three Japanese boys laughing and splashing as they waited to catch a wave. Hogan caught a big one and rode it through the gap in the fringing reef, his face and body hidden in white foam. I could see at its end that he was exhilarated by the ride. When he picked himself from the surf, I yelled, "God will punish you."

The Japanese gang leader gave me his usual deadpan look, grabbed his board, and started out to sea. "I'm YBA," Hogan yelled as he kicked the water. God didn't punish Hogan for his wickedness and what did he mean, "I'm YBA"?

I trotted over to Raymond's house. He was two years older and wiser than I. "What's YBA?"

Raymond said, "Young Buddhist Association. Their temple is right on the highway next to Waitala swamp."

"How come God doesn't punish them for surfing?"

"They're not Christians."

Here was a conundrum. "I thought everybody believed in God."

Raymond shook his head. "The Japanese do not." Then he showed me a picture of four bronze-skinned men leaning on twelve-foot-tall surfboards. Pointing to one man, whose board had "Duke" written on it, he said, "Kahanamoku surfs. God doesn't punish him."

I was young and naïve, but I learned from Raymond's explanation that if a man named Duke could ride the waves, if Hogan and his gang could do the same and the sky did not fall on any of them, then what should I be afraid of?

I scurried home and consulted my best friend, Sooky Fernandes. No relation. He has the "s" I have the "z" on the end. Why the difference? I do not know. It is confusing because the "z" is the Spanish spelling for Fernandez, but I am Portuguese. For years some people thought I came from Spain.

"Sooky, ask your father if Catholics can surf."

He nodded and we parted company.

For a day I waited impatiently for an answer.

Finally Sooky came back. "He said yes."

In all this turmoil you might ask why I didn't consult my father. Because I knew his answer: "The only good boy is a hard working boy." I had to find a way to get the answer I wanted. I needed a reliable source to approve of an act that might be equated with laziness. When scolded by my dad, I could say, "Frank Fernandes said I could do it."

Reinforced by this approval of our surfing plan, Sooky and I set about preparing to challenge the waves. In my time it's not an easy task. The only true surfboards were twelve-to-fourteen-foot monsters of solid koa. They were so heavy that it took two men to carry a surfboard to the water. Nor did I have money to buy one. I noticed that Hogan and his gang surfed with a washboard or an ironing board. Both had flat surfaces that are not tapered like the curved shape of a boat.

The ironing board appeared the best choice. It had a rounded prow and my skinny body could fit on top of it. But how was I to get one?

Luckily, my mother discarded a board. Retrieving it from the wood pile, I started the slow process of pulling out all the tacks fastening the cloth wrapped around the wood. Split at the top, I nailed a wooden bar across its width. The bar served two purposes, holding the piece of wood together, and allowing me to grasp the board's prow and steer it once I caught the wave.

It's not easy to do this work. I needed help constructing my surfboard and got it from my friend Raymond. I did not want to let my father know what I was doing for fear he would stop the project. Mind you, even though I practiced *mahapi,* I still did my daily chores.

Finally the right day arrived. The tide rolled in with big waves smashing over a hundred- yard-long rock barrier that rose twenty feet from shore. This craggy formation of thrust-up stone created a natural lagoon that children could safely swim in. But the waves that smash over the barrier and ripple toward the shore are too puny for surfing.

Near the north end of this wall were two gaps, one three feet and the second, twenty feet wide. To surf, I paddled out through the widest gap to reach the bigger breaking waves. It's not easy, for the ironing board barely supported my weight. Stroking was not an option, rather kicking and pushing off the reef bottom was necessary to get to the spot where the waves broke. With my heart thumping and my lungs gasping air, Sooky and I swam out of the lagoon into the deeper blue water.

"Watch out for the eels," Hogan yelled. His friends laughed as they saw our panic. There was another worry. Our parents had forbidden passing the lagoon barrier. "Too dangerous," my mother said. "The currents can sweep you out to sea." Raymond had warned, "A hammerhead shark makes his home in the channel near the surfing spot. It can smell blood a mile away and come for dinner." I checked my body to make sure I was not bleeding.

Hogan took off on a wave, screaming. Seawater washed over me, nearly tearing the ironing board from my grasp. What to do? How do you catch a wave?

I watched the Japanese boys. Saw them wait until the water began to swell, then they pushed off from the bottom, kicking hard to achieve the same forward momentum as the wave.

Hogan returned from his ride. "Plenty oysters. Watch out. Wave makes you pearl dive." I ignored his jibe.

A big swell came, tall as a house. Its roar sent stabs of fear through my body. My bare feet pushed off the reef. I kicked hard, but the front of my board dipped down as the wave curled. Surging water thrust me to the bottom like an arrow shot from a bow. Chunking into the reef, the ironing board flipped and I hurtled over the rocks into the lagoon.

Gasping, I struggled to the surface believing I had been underwater for an eternity and I barely escaped drowning. My ironing board bobbed in the lagoon. Coral cuts lacerated my chest and legs. They started to bleed.

Beside me, Sooky said, "We quit."

Should I take his advice? Grab my board and drag it on the sand and head home? Did I dare go out again and risk the hammerhead? He would smell blood and come hunting. On the other hand, Hogan would call me a coward. He would tease me forever and say, "Japanese boys are better than Hawaiians."

"But," I argued to myself, "Hawaiians invented surfing. I'm half-Hawaiian. I can do it." Despite the black-finned monster that lurked somewhere in the channel, I pushed out of the lagoon and into the open sea. Foolish? Yes, for Sooky had more sense than I and left for home.

With my feet bouncing off the reef bottom to keep my head above water, I waited for the right wave. My eyes strayed towards the channel a hundred yards away. I searched for a fin knifing through the sea. I had been told, "When the shark comes, smack the water hard with your hands. The noise will frighten it away." I prayed that *mano* would not come. I did not want to test this claim.

Water swelled as a wave built up behind me. I pushed off the reef, kicked hard, and clutched the parallel bar that helps me keep the nose of my craft up. Surging water pushed my board. It began to pearl dive. I slid backwards, my feet dangling, and my hands vainly trying to keep the prow above water. Surrounded by foam, I hurtled through the twenty-foot break in the reef coasting into shore. Exhilarating, exciting, fantastic, I thought. I lifted my ironing board above my head like a conquering hero.

Again, and yet again, I went out to challenge the waves. I forgot all about *mano* as I learned to love surfing. Then Hogan pricked my balloon.

"You can't do *this*," Hogan challenged as he caught a wave and headed straight for the three-foot gap in the reef, He disappeared from sight as sea water smashed into the rock barrier creating mounds of foam. He is dead, I thought.

But after many seconds Hogan rose, splashed his hand in the lagoon, and teased, "Nah. Nah, you can't do what I did."

Oh, such an insufferable challenge. A hard headed *katonk* dared me to do something crazy. Should I accept? I had survived pearl diving, escaped drowning, and so far the hammerhead shark. If I came home all broken from crashing into the lagoon wall, it would be the stick and a permanent grounding. Hogan and his friends laughed at my indecision.

"Scaredy cat. Scaredy cat," they teased.

I eyed the narrow gap like a golfer preparing for a long putt into a tiny hole. This is my first try at surfing. I am a novice, not a daredevil. Only a fool would chance the threading of the narrow gap. Couldn't my tormentors cut me some slack? But like all first-timers, this is their means of testing you to see if you are afraid to try. If I failed to meet the challenge I would be forever branded as chicken. I gulped, thinking that everything in life seemed sweet and sour.

A wave built up behind me, rising to huge heights. It lifted the end of the board as I kicked off from the reef bottom. Instead of holding the bar, I held the sides of the ironing board to guide it through the narrow gap. I splashed with my thin legs. My feet did not give me the power I needed. I stroked hard with my right hand. My board tilted sideways. If I slid off, this daring venture would end in a debacle. My body would smash into the reef to be cut and broken. Panic rose as my craft sped at the stone barrier. Surging water hid the gap. Saltwater blinded me. For a moment I saw the opening and kicked for it. The wave pushed me into the tiny gap, my board bumping its edges, scraping my fingers. I fought my panic. Like a miracle from heaven I found myself in the quiet waters of the lagoon.

I rose, staring at Hogan. Then I picked up my ironing board and trudged along the sand, heading home.

* * *

"Poi My Boy Will Make A Man of You" was a popular song during my growing up years. Weaned on this purple-grey starch, I loved poi, especially since I thought it would make me strong. Despite this claim, any visitors who came to the island gagged when they saw the thick, goopy paste. There was a belief among these newcomers that poi is an evil concoction designed to make you sick.

But consider for a moment the importance of this vegetable to the survival of the Polynesians. From this plant and its light, bulb-shaped root came all the nutrients for human survival. Even more significant to a boy, it was the only paste that we had. Poi is sticky and when glue was needed to hold things together, young, thick poi was the best.

Near my home, where a bluff of land juts into the sea and the cannery waste disposal pipe empties the pineapple trash into the water, was the greatest kite flying spot on the island. The Japanese and Chinese taught the rest of us the thrill of flying paper into the sky.

Friend Raymond taught me how to make a kite. Bamboo strips were laid in a cross. String wrapped at their joinder and fastened across the ends to form a diamond. Paper was laid over the bamboo skeleton, bent over the strings, and then glued with fresh, thick poi. Once the paste was dry, a cord was attached to bow the kite, followed by strips of cloth to give the craft flying stability.

Off to the bluff with a spool of string and in the sharp breezes sweeping over the sand, I watched my kite soar into a sky filled with massive clouds flowing across the ocean. Oh, it was fun to cause it to turn left or right, swoop, then fight the wind as it sought to gain height. Sometimes the kite, despite my tugging, failed to rise and came crashing to the scrub grass covering the ground. No matter the failure, I picked up the poi-glued bird and let it fly again.

But it was not peace and tranquility on the windy ground. Onto the bluff swaggered Hogan with a rice paper kite. It was colorful with a painted picture of a fiery dragon. Off into the brooding overcast it flew into the sky.

I looked at my pitiful newspaper-covered kite held together by poi and was shamed by the superior craft soaring above me. Still, I had to see if I could meet the challenge and I ran along the flat ground, forcing my kite into the sky. Fresh wind grasped it and the vessel soared up. The updraft flung it higher and my string sizzled as it unwound from my spool. The kite flew so high that it seemed to be the height of Wai'ale'ale Mountain, whose rippling pond at the top was shrouded in heavy clouds. It is the wettest spot on earth. The constant deluge of rain overflows its crater and cascades in silver strings of water along its blue-green side. I am awed by its mile-high height and massive size. It's a place where ancient Hawaiians would climb to make sacrifices to the gods and seek *mana*, spiritual power.

Rudely, my dreaming was shattered as I felt a sharp tug on my string. The dragon was striking my kite, puncturing a hole in the newsprint. "What's going on?" I yelled.

"It's war," answered Hogan, maneuvering his flying rice-paper beast in a second assault on my wounded craft.

My kite began to flutter. I yelled at my enemy, "What you got on the end?"

"A nail. Surrender?"

"No way." It was an empty claim, for my kite had no weapon and was inferior in quality to the flying dragon. The only course of action was to run away and live to fight another day. I raced to the beach, hoping that Hogan could not follow. But my foe was undaunted. He pursued me with the painted flame-breathing beast seeking to devour my puny kite.

Avoiding running in a straight line, I climbed the sand dunes and began a weaving run toward Waitala, a dark pool that is the home of evil creatures. Maybe Hogan would give up when he got near this devil-filled murky pond.

But my opponent was relentless as he pursued me towards the edge of this abyss that harbors everything that is frightful. I dare not get close for fear that I will slide down Waitala's steep side. I can't head back to the beach, for my kite will lose the wind, fall, and Hogan will win. Heading towards Wai'ale'ale was my only hope, but the berm of the railroad track loomed above me. I knew it would be difficult to climb it.

Sensing my purpose, Hogan raced toward the high ground where he could easily dive- bomb my kite. Escaping the threat seemed hopeless. Still, I struggled up the rising ground toward the railroad tracks. Hogan achieved the crest first and I saw him begin the sharp tug on the kite string that would force the dragon into its victorious dive.

"Clang, clang," a train bell bellowed its warning of the approach of a black iron locomotive with its rattling cars filled with freshly cut cane. I welcomed the sound of the clanking chains that bound the burnt sugar stalks to the rail wagons. Retreating toward the ocean, my kite fluttered, but managed to stay aloft.

Hogan was startled by the onrush of the train and slid down the berm. The slackened kite line caused the paper dragon to lose height.

My foe escaped the rush of the charging engine, but his falling craft was not so lucky. It snagged onto the iron engine and was torn by it.

Hogan wound in the wreck of his kite.

Mine was still aloft. "I win," I cried, running with my kite along the bluff. It was not in my nature to be sportsmanlike. After all, I did not seek out this war.

CHAPTER 2

Sharing

In my home, food was always on the table. Vegetables, rice, poi and some type of main dish like meat or fish. I hated green things, tomatoes, and carrots. For many minutes, I would poke at my food and was told if I didn't eat my vegetables there would be no dessert. Making a face, I shoveled in a morsel then attacked the main dish. Again the parental admonishment, "Eat everything on your plate. Waste nothing, think of all the starving people in China."

To this day, I eat what is on my plate starting with the vegetables, the dish I once hated. Whether there are people starving in China, I do not know. But the Chinese in Kapa'a did not starve. How did those living in our small town manage to survive? The coastal steamer seldom came with food to eat.

The answer was simple: the multiple races on Kaua'i lived in the traditional Hawaiian way, sharing and trading. We had a vegetable garden, fruit trees, a chicken and duck yard, and a home-made incubator for baby chicks. There were many days where I would tend to the chicken eggs, keeping them warm with a kerosene lantern, then, when fuzzy yellow balls hatched, making sure the tiny ones were fed. Healthy young chickens were easy to sell or barter with.

When I needed clothes, my mother would give me material from Shido Store and a dozen eggs, sending me to Mrs. Urabe, the Japanese seamstress three houses down the street. The old mama-san made me pants in exchange for eggs or papayas or a chicken.

Chinese loved "stink eggs," duck eggs soaked in brine for a month or more. The longer they were submerged the darker the color of the eggs. Once black enough they were easy to trade for sweet pork or Peking Duck.

I remember walking with a parent to a local rice patch with trade goods. A small shack stood centered in a large rectangular pond of water. Thin green reeds grew in long neat rows beside it.

"Kapow," a shotgun blasted, followed by the yanking of cords fanning from the shack over the rice field. Hundreds of tin cans attached to the cords smashed into each other. Cawing in protest, dark-colored mynah birds flew from the pond. These pests can demolish acres of planted rice if allowed to feast without being frightened away by noise.

In a field nearby a young boy yoked to a wooden plow pulled it through the earth, creating furrowed ground for planting. In the course of trading you learned that rice farmers had a tough life. They worked by hand with primitive tools. From sunrise to sunset, the farm family toiled, growing their crops and struggling to save them from predators. I did not want to be a rice farmer. But I was told that the Japanese plow boy was "a very good boy. You should work like that boy." No way, I would much rather clean up the chicken poop and dig it into the garden than be harnessed to a plow pulling it through a field.

We did have a chicken and duck farm with many females, a rooster, and a drake. Any more males would have led to warfare where only one would survive.

You must watch a rooster in a chicken yard. The crafty fowl knew my sex. If my eyes strayed from him, the animal would attack. It was a good reason for carrying a stick when feeding the flightless birds. Why he was jealous is beyond me. He had a harem of thirty hens. They didn't need protection from me.

A rooster with a reluctant hen is interesting to watch. The male bird would chase the female around the yard. She dodges, squawks and weaves, trying to escape. But at some point she slows down and is caught. The rooster leaps on her back, grabs her neck with his beak, and stabs his body down a few times, making a deposit.

The drake had it much easier. Female ducks are plump and can't waddle very fast. A leap, a love bite on the top of the neck, a deposit and the job was done. After this momentous event the female duck was proud of these seconds of romance. Her neck thrusts back and forth. Her wings ruffle and flap. Then she plods along the sand of the duck yard quacking like a proud parent to be.

This is a birds and bees story. But in my naïveté, I believed that I had been brought to my parents by a stork. For adults did not act like animals. Later in life the truth would be revealed to me.

Every evening I chased the hens and rooster into a three-sided hutch. Despite their complaints they complied, leaping onto perches high above the floor. Somehow they knew that danger came in the darkness. I lowered a screen grate sealing their hovel, and hoped that the predators would not find their way in. In the past, we had lost a covey of doves to rats.

Days passed without incident until there came a night filled with the screams of domesticated birds. Wild cackling woke the house. I rushed outside in pajamas, heading for the hen coop. My father yelled, "Get inside." He dashed by me, a kerosene lantern in his hand. Disobedient because I was curious, I followed him to the scene of the pandemonium.

Through the lathe gate closing the fenced pen, the pale light of the lantern revealed fowl scattering about. My father held something in his hand. He pushed open the gate. Under a chicken coop the flaming light glinted from red eyes, the rest of the animal's body hidden in darkness. I knew the rat was big.

"In the house," my mother said, spanking my bottom.

I edged from the battle, watching my parents enter the yard. I wondered if the devil had come to steal the chickens. Animals screeched, my father yelled, "Two of them." Sounds of combat filled the night with noise. I couldn't sleep until my parents returned to the house complaining of rats.

In the morning the family surveyed the damage. A passel of scavengers had worked their way through the lathe fencing. They succeeded in tearing apart two ducks and attacked the chicken house. I can still remember a duck, his chest torn, and his heart beating as it fought to live. The wounded had to be put down, the hole in the fence mended and reinforced with chicken wire.

What has all this to do with sharing? It explains the lessons you learn from raising animals for trade. They must be fed and protected. Predators are present and it is your job to make sure your flock survives. Negligence, by not keeping a break in the fence repaired, was costly. If you have lost what can be sold then you will starve. The boat seldom comes to Kaua'i with food to eat. It made no difference. We didn't have money to buy what did come in.

Being the bearer of trade goods allowed entry into shops that I would not otherwise have been invited to. I can still recall a great blue eagle plastered on the wall of an auto repair shop. Above this fearsome bird were the words: NRA member. In the garage, several men whispered. I heard the words, "end of unions...take down...plantations no like."

One man said, "What's this kid doing here?"

The owner of the shop turned to me saying, "Bobby, out of here before the cops come."

I scooted away, frightened and puzzled. Why were these men meeting in secret? What were they afraid of? What's a union? Why did the plantations want to arrest the people in the garage?

A few days later I peeped into the shop. The blue bird poster had disappeared. The garage owner muttered, "Court ended the NRA." A force powerful as God had struck down the mighty eagle.

CHAPTER 3

Sabidong

"Puff-a-gee-gee, puff-a-gee-gee," chanted my two-year-old cousin hopping from foot to foot. I held his hand tight, otherwise he would run to catch the black locomotive pulling twenty rail cars of cut sugar cane. Clouds of belching steam spewed into the air as the big engine hauled the product of a day's labor by scores of Filipino men.

A couple of older boys reached out to grasp dangling stalks of burnt cane from the wheeled boxes rushing past us. A dangerous pursuit, for the snatcher could be pulled under the steel rollers by an unyielding stalk. But risk of death or maiming was never a consideration. Racing alongside the train and pulling out a branch of sweet burnt sugar cane from a high piled stack was akin to a victory in a race. This accomplishment was followed by peeling the rind and strutting along the railroad track munching the sweet cane. It was akin to the feeling a wide receiver has when he snatches from the sky a winning touchdown.

Sugar cane fields carpeted the arable land of the island from the ocean to the low hills. When a field was eighteen months old it would be set afire. Flames and dense smoke filled the sky. Rats by the hundreds scurried from the burning forest. Once the embers cooled, workmen swung machetes into the leafless branches of cane, chopping the stems but leaving the roots to allow the plants to grow again. Severed stalks were manhandled into waiting rail cars.

Loaded trains hauled the harvest to the sugar mill on rail tracks that ran by the homes of families living in Kapa'a. Safety of people was a minor consideration. Sugar was king and the rail tracks were laid where the train could easily haul the burnt cuttings to the mill.

Along both sides of the main highway belting the island grew thousands of acres of sugar cane. Fences and gates barred entry to the fields to all except plantation workmen. Posted on some enclosures might be a sign: *Sabidong.* Painted beneath it was a skull and crossbones. It was a warning to rascals like me that death awaited those who trespassed into plantation property. This prohibition often prevented access to the sea.

In the 1930s Kaua'i had several sugar mills. Their prime features were the camps, each housing a distinct race, the sugar mill, and the company store. Strict regulations regimented the living conditions of the workers. The imported laborer was expected to purchase his needs from the company store, charging what he bought against earnings. Often a worker owed more to the plantation than he earned.

By contrast, Kapa'a did not have its beginnings as a plantation camp. Its growth came from Chinese who saw in the marshland on the west edge of its boundaries an opportunity to grow rice. Their efforts produced wealth for themselves and developed a community. The vestiges of rice growing were still apparent in the 1930s: a rice storage house, Chinese workers living in bunk houses, and Chinese merchants operating stores.

What moved Kapa'a from a Chinese community into a town of all races was James Dole. This entrepreneur, styling himself as the "Pineapple King", started the industry in Hawai'i. In 1913 Hawaiian Pineapple opened a cannery in Kapa'a. Hundreds came to the community to help grow, harvest,

and can the fruit. Other hundreds came to provide services for these workers. The result was a multi-ethnic town consisting of Hawaiians and the
people who had been imported to work in the sugar fields.

In contrast to the labor camps of the plantations, with their rules for
waking, working, socializing, and sleeping, the citizens of Kapa'a owned
their homes. This fact allowed them to live in freedom. Important to the
town was its eastern boundary the Pacific Ocean. There were no fences,
Sabidong signs, or plantation watchmen that prevented us from enjoying
the sea and harvesting its products.

Still, the restrictions to ocean access had significance. A mile north of
Kapa'a was a mill, Kealia, and beyond it were sugar fields covering the land
from the sea to the foothills. A railroad girdled the coastline.

The shore beyond Kealia was rugged with huge black boulders and
steep cliffs. But it was a treasure trove of shellfish. An *opihi* hunter, like me,
waited for the right day and low tide when the surf did not pound the coast
with awesome waves.

Such a day arrived and with my friend Ambrose, we trudged along
the sand to the black rim of boulders edging the cliff coastline of Kealia.
The sun peeped over the horizon shining on gentle waves washing over
the beach. We easily scurried along the rocks close to the water, harvesting
opihi. With such a superb day, shellfish hunting was easy and we lost track
of time and tide until the ocean surged around our feet, legs, and hips.

No matter, we scampered along the rocks like crabs seeking higher
ground. But *opihi* loves to be dashed with waves, for that was how they get
nutrients to grow big. Hence the largest of these shellfish are closest to the
pounding sea. We must work near the wash of the water to find our best
prizes.

When the occasional locomotive chugged by, we hid within the rocks.
We believed that the plantations controlled the land to the edge of the
sea and we dared not be seen by the trainmen. Once the last car passed we
continued the hunt.

With harvest bags full, it was time to return home, but *auwe* (too bad)
the sea had become angry. Monster waves crashed along the coastline. They
made our trip along the black boulders perilous.

What to do? Climb to the railroad tracks and walk along the right of
way? That was dangerous. The engineer might not see us.

From a distance, over the waving leaves of cane rustling in the wind, came the thin sound of chugging. The main road was nearby. But the sugar field stood dense and seven feet high. It appeared ready for burning. What about *Sabidong,* the poison spray of death? Except for shorts we were naked. Would we shrivel and die as we forced our way through the cane forest?

Ambrose said, "Look for plantation road."

Shivering, I answered, "Run along the track."

We hopped from tie to tie, trying to avoid the cinders between the wooden crossbeams that anchored the rails. Our toughened bare feet could be punctured by the slender splintered rocks.

"Train coming," said a nervous Ambrose.

"No stop. Keep going," I said, my heart pounding and fear mounting. It was not fright of the train or *Sabidong* that caused me to be afraid, but the knowledge that if my mother knew the hole we had dug ourselves into, the spanking would be severe.

"Train coming. I see the steam."

"Not steam. Waves pounding rocks."

"Dirt road."

We dashed into the opening in the forest of cane stalks.

"Hang low," I cautioned, "so nobody see us. Jump into the field if somebody comes."

"You crazy? What about *Sabidong?*" Ambrose said.

"Take the chance, better than jail," I answered.

Ahead of us, the road ended in a gate. Just beyond was the main highway. Wow, we made it. But then a dark figure stepped out of the cane field.

My heart pounded into my throat. My legs weakened and I couldn't move. The Filipino man had a huge cane knife in his hand. Run into the field? Run back to the shoreline? But maybe we were surrounded by Filipino men with knives? Reputation had it that they were the best in knife cutting.

We stopped dead, whispering, "What to do?"

The field worker wearing a long sleeved shirt, dark pants, and heavy black boots stared at us as we kicked up dirt with our feet, ashamed that we had been caught trespassing. He said something in Ilocano, a dialect from northern Luzon in the Philippine Islands. I did not understand him. He waved his cane knife and I thought he meant to take us prisoner. Surrender seemed the only option left. Oh, would there be a thrashing tonight.

Stumbling to the gate, the Filipino gave a gold-toothed smile. He pushed open the barrier and waved us onto the highway.

You had to feel sorry for these men. They were imported without wives or children and without any prospects of ever having a family in Hawai'i. I always found that they were especially kind to young local boys. Maybe it was because they were lonely and pined for family.

CHAPTER 4

The Raft

"Mister, Auntie say you teach swimming," I said, staring at Smokey Louie towering over me.

"Easy," answered the life guard. The early morning sun shone on his bronze body and its well-oiled skin. Louie was built like Charles Atlas, the muscle guy who moved trains with his teeth. He got his name "Smokey" for the cigars he loved to inhale.

Draping me over his knees, the life guard said, "You paddle with your hands like this." Smokey demonstrated a crawl. "Then kick with your feet like this." Louie waved my feet up and down.

A big wave came rushing toward shore. Louie lifted me by my shorts and said, "Swim."

Heaved over the wave, water covered me. Pawing like a frightened dog, I fought my way to the surface gasping for air. All prior water experiences had been accomplished with my feet touching the bottom. This time I was in panic mode. I couldn't touch anything except water.

Slapping and kicking the sea to stay afloat, I failed to realize that salt water is more buoyant than fresh water and all you need to do was keep your head above it. Try it. Roll on your back in the ocean and you can float for hours. At least if there aren't big waves.

Hands, arms, feet pushing into the sea, I stayed afloat. The waves rolled me in. Rising from the sand, I glanced at Smokey. I had nearly drowned and he was laughing.

"Hey, Tommy," Louie said. He called every kid Tommy. "You can swim."

Louie's teaching method was life threatening and useless. But that was the way it was in the old days, sink or swim. Coaching didn't exist. Sports equipment didn't exist. You made what you needed or went without.

The County of Kaua'i provided one good thing for youngsters, a wooden raft lashed to fifty-gallon drums and anchored in deep water off shore. It was a place where you could dangle your feet in the sea, do daredevil dives, or play king of the hill. That game on a raft was dangerous with shoving, wrestling, and pushing heads under water. Older, bigger boys loved doing that to small fry like me.

Despite the threat of combat, getting to the County raft was a reason to learn to swim. Once proficient at keeping my head above water, I pushed out to sea and the raft bobbing in the blue water a hundred feet from shore. I swam like Johnny Weissmuller, my head above water and staring straight ahead. Feet and arms shoving into the sea like a dog seeking a safe harbor, I inched to the raft. Then the combats began. A fat Hawaiian kid called Moki was king. He knocked my hand from the platform while shoving my head under water. A fifty-gallon drum slammed into me. Desperation set in. I am tired, gulping water. Where was Smokey? Isn't he the lifeguard? Isn't he supposed to stop this mayhem?

But pretty girls sauntered along the beach. They distracted Louie from his duties as he strutted about like a peacock showing off his muscles.

Deep breath, kick under the bobbing raft into the open space between drums. Look between the wooden planks for a spot where Moki isn't. Push off for the unguarded area, and slither onto the raft. Once on, you had a chance. I grabbed Moki's leg.

"Eh, let go or bust you up."

A hard pull and the fat kid toppled backward, smacking the platform. Today, my bones would break, but young bodies are like new rubber easily bouncing back from a hard fall.

Moki came up ready to hand wrestle, but another kid, tired of his dominance, shoved him into the water. The two of us controlled the raft and held off all comers until a truce was made. With peace on the raft, I dangled my feet in the sea watching a bright sun sparkle on waves rolling into shore. There were no surf riders or canoe paddlers on the water. Such frivolity was *de rigueur*, frowned upon. Besides, canoes and surfboards were expensive to build and the right trees had to be imported from another island. None could afford that.

Instead of having the equipment to ride the sea, I had the freedom to enjoy the beauty of the mountains rising beyond the beach. On this day they were dark blue-green and cloudless Waterfalls plunged down the steep flanks of Wai'ale'ale, the extinct volcano that had created Kaua'i. This massive mound of rock had spewed from a crack in the crust of the earth five hundred thousand years ago. The lava emitting from its snout pushed from the deep, rising in huge waves of rapidly cooling stone, seventeen thousand feet to reach the surface of the sea.

Billions of pounds of rock spewed onto the ocean, creating a unique island sixty-four miles around and twenty-five-hundred miles from any continent. Wai'ale'ale's fires went dormant as the crack in the earth moved southeast creating, more land. Today, there are twelve volcanic islands that we call Hawai'i. Kilauea volcano is still angry. It spews lava in waves, making the biggest island in the chain larger every year.

This was my homeland, a tropical island where it rains constantly. This gift of water makes the land green, gloriously fresh, and beautiful. I thought of this as I watched waterfalls speeding down the flank of fifty-two-hundred-feet high Wai'ale'ale Mountain.

Along the shore, palm trees rustled in the warm air. The raft swayed in the surging waves like a rocking chair. Its sealed iron drums spanked the water in a rhythmic chop-chop. The sounds of the sea were mesmerizing and peaceful until Moki yelled, "Shark!"

Those who have seen the movie *Jaws* will understand the heart-pounding fear that the word conveys to a six-year-old. All the pictures I had ever seen of that animal were of gaping jaws filled with jagged teeth. Sharp fangs poised like hundreds of daggers ready to rend, tear, and feast on flesh.

"Where?" I said, struggling to breathe. My heart throbbed, pushing out from my chest like a bellows. Out of the water came feet and hands. I scurried to the center of the raft, searching the sea for the fins of mano.

The big ones will show two, one of them a tail fin. When the fish is ready to strike, the tail whips the water like the blur of a windmill churning in a stiff breeze.

But there were no fins knifing the water. Nor was there the long dark shape of the devil fish speeding toward the raft.

A false alarm?

Moki was tricky. Nasty guy, he shoved me into the water crowing, "Man-eater coming for you."

I had read of Jesus walking on water and for a brief moment I tried to do that. Hands, feet, flailing, I fought to the surface and struggled to get back on the raft. Although the sea is buoyant I could not achieve water-walking speed. Nor could I get on the raft with a grinning Moki ready to shove me back in. My feet began to sink as I tired from all my struggling. I thought the end had come, and if I had to go into the tummy of the shark, Moki would join me. As he reached down to push me under, I seized his hand and pulled. His splash and shriek is still vivid and satisfying to this day.

When he surfaced, Moki laughed, saying, "No shark."

"Oh yeah, well, look behind you."

When he turned, I pulled myself onto the raft, exhausted.

The ocean around our refuge of planks and fifty-gallon drums rolled in, marred by waves cresting in foaming caps of white. Shark fins were absent. Children and adults splashed in the shallow water along the beach. Moki stroked toward the raft offering his hand in a gesture of peace. I took it. He pulled me into the water and squiggled into my place on the raft, saying, "You big sucker."

That was how it was in the old days, lots of harmless horseplay. But as I floated on my back heading to the shore, I vowed that someday I would overcome my fear of mano and swim underwater to see the wonders of the deep and the thousands of fish who lived and thrived along the reef. Let the shark come. I'd bang him on his nose. Take out my knife and tangle with the beast. With those brave thoughts I made the shore, trudged up the sand, and reported to my aunt how I had learned to swim.

* * *

Being able to stay afloat with a dog-like stroke meant that I could travel to swimming holes hidden in the mountains. The magic word was Waipahee. A mountain pool with a thirty- foot moss-covered rockslide carved out of the rock by a stream plunging from the high ground.

Cousins Stanford, Pono, and Alice spoke of the pool as if it was a wonder of the world. They created an excitement to experience the slide into a deep pond. You couldn't visit it at any time. Sundays were best since the plantations would not be working the sugar cane fields. But more important, you had to wait for the right day, when clouds did not ring the mountains. If their ridges were hidden in mist, beware of what might come.

My imagination magnified the stories I had heard of ghosts who thrived in clouded hills. Out of them came spooks who seized and dragged you away. Or warriors of the lost tribe snuck from their villages to choose you for human sacrifice. I shivered as I thought of it. I felt the knife slipping into my body, cutting out my heart to be devoured by the cannibals. Were these tales true or just stories designed to keep wayward children close to the family?

A Sunday dawned with the air crisp and the sky blue. Mountain flanks loomed dark green, their seldom-seen tips swept clear of clouds. "After church," my aunt announced, "we go to Waipahee." My parents and sister were on the continent studying movie theaters. I was left to live with relatives. The elders of the family considered the mainland too dangerous for an unpredictable kid who flitted about like a mosquito.

With thoughts of the slippery slide racing in my mind, I blotted out the drudgery of the Catholic ritual. I kneeled, stood, and prayed, mimicking the actions of the adults in front of me. When the service ended, I wiggled through the crowd standing outside of the church, hopping from one foot to the other as the adults jabbered like mynah birds with their friends.

Sooky, my pal and former neighbor, came to me saying, "Where you been?"

"Living in Kapa'a. Hey, we're going to Waipahee, the slippery slide. Want to come?"

"No. Too dangerous. I can't go. See you."

The family crammed into a black four-door Ford. Pono set the solenoids. Stanford pulled the crank creating the spark that fired up the engine. We jugged into the hills following a winding road to the turnoff at the stone monument to Colonel Spaulding, founder of the Kealia Sugar Plantation. We left the rutted macadam road, our car motoring onto a dirt pathway still damp from a heavy rain the night before. We slalomed along its surface. Pono kept the vehicle close to the middle, avoiding the shallow ditches to each side of the roadway. If we slid into one of them, the wheels would mire in mud, and our adventure would end.

I've experienced being stuck in the mud. When it occurs, the passengers exit the car, find logs, and wedge them under the tires. Everyone except the driver aligns behind and alongside the trapped auto. The driver guns the engine. We push. If you are lucky, the wheels find traction and the auto spins out of the cloying earth, splattering the pushers with mud. But if the tires do not grasp the timber, it's a disaster. The car sinks to its axles and all hope of escaping the muck is over. What follows is a long trek home and a search for help.

Pono was an expert driver and he piloted our auto skillfully along the plantation road. But there was trouble ahead, a steep grade. We abandoned the auto. In first gear, the Ford moved up the hill. Sugar cane stalks rustled in the slight breeze. A mountain dark with shadow loomed ahead. We were alone in this forbidding place. Excitement from the early morning evaporated. Sooky's words rang in my ears, "Too dangerous." Maybe we should turn back while we still can.

A loud "pop" from the exhaust roused me from my morbid thoughts. I saw the Ford cresting the rise and reaching firm ground. "Come on," called Stanford, "or we'll leave you behind."

Pulling myself from the muck I sloshed my way to the car, only to be scolded by Aunt Katie, "Clean your feet."

With a burlap sack I wiped away the mud and hopped in. Our car chugged ahead, the tires finding good traction on the pathway. Within minutes, Pono pulled into a rock-strewn glade. Tufts of grass peeped through the stones. The mountain towered above me. A thin wisp of cloud drifted along its flank. Bordering the flat ground stood a dense jungle of guava trees appearing to deny any access to Waipahee.

Picnic baskets were handed out. "Come," said Stanford, leading the way into the thicket. Parting the branches, I followed him down stone steps into a ravine lined with boulders. Rushing water smashed the rocks and somewhere below I could hear the sound of whooping and hollering.

Fear fled as I rushed ahead. "Wait for us," Aunt Katie called.

But I was too excited to stop. I raced to the edge of black rocks that jutted over a chasm and looked down on an emerald pool shimmering below me. A shrieking boy slid down a moss-covered slide, plunged into the water, and disappeared. Water cascaded along the chute flowing like a wide open spigot into the pond.

Where was the boy? I wondered. Then I saw him kicking up from the deep. He popped to the surface, his face wreathed in a smile. He swam to the rock edge of the pool and began to climb.

"Come on. Let's go," Pono said as he splashed to the edge then, head first, let the water drag him into the slide. With hands extended in front, Pono knifed into the pool, barely rippling the surface. I understood what Sooky meant by "dangerous."

Shivering with indecision I stood by the water slide.

"Come on, kid," someone yelled. "You're holding up the parade."

I looked behind me. Two boys snickered, saying, "Chicken."

Goaded, I stepped into the water, waded to the edge, closed my eyes and plunged. "Whoa! Whoa!" I yelled, trying to slow my speed with my hands. But the moss was too slick. I smashed into the water with a loud splash.

Plunging feet first into a mountain pool was exhilarating. Few experiences in life can equal it. For the next hour I could not stop sliding, swimming, climbing, and sliding again. I only stopped when ordered to eat lunch.

I swallowed my *ume*-laced rice ball and teriyaki meat and within minutes stood ready to slide again. But I was ordered to rest. "You will get a cramp in your stomach," Aunt Katie said.

"You cramp in the water," Stanford added, "you die."

I scoffed at this sinister prediction, but obeyed.

The delay ended the fun of the day. The grownups cast suspicious eyes on the dark clouds building on the mountain top. A light drizzle fell.

"We go," Katie said.

"Why?" I protested, kicking the ground.

"Maybe flash flood coming. Fill this valley with water."

Suddenly, I understood the danger of this beautiful place. We trudged uphill. Piled into the Ford and drove away. Wistfully, I gazed at the receding Eden of Waipahee. Today it is closed to all visitors. For me, the childhood experiences still linger and I would want to try once more the slippery slide.

CHAPTER 5

The Solid

"What a sickening smell," I said, trudging along the railroad track heading over the bridge spanning the dark pond of Waitala.

My Hawaiian friend, Ambrose Worthington, nodded his head. "They grinding," confirming what we both knew, that the canning season had begun.

Kapa'a had gotten its start from a king who thought he could become rich as a sugar planter. Kalakaua and a whaling captain, James Makee, established a sugar mill on the north end of town about the time that General George Armstrong Custer was annihilated at the battle of the Little Bighorn. Makee died within a year of starting the mill. The king and his cronies were failures as sugar growers and the enterprise collapsed. A thrifty, hard-working Chinese took over the shanties that had been built by royalty and planted rice in the marshland on the west edge of Kapa'a town. Other Chinese immigrants left the indentured servitude of the highly regulated white-owned sugar plantations and joined the man.

Unlike the Hawaiian king's courtiers, the Chinese were hard working and understood rice growing. Despite living hand to mouth, the enterprising men prospered. They built a rice mill, warehouse, homes, and merchant shops in the strip of firm ground between the ocean and the marshland. (Kapa'a means "the solid.")

These early entrepreneurs accounted for the strong Chinese presence in my town. This was evident as Ambrose and I kicked up dust from the Government Road walking past the Hee Fat building, Chun Kin's Tailor Shop, and Young Bong's Store. But there were others beside the Chinese who made a home in Kapa'a.

A year before the Great War, the Hawaiian Pineapple Company built a huge metal enclosed cannery at the edge of town. Many miles to the north, beneath the pointed ridges of Anahola Mountain, acres of land were cleared, cultivated and planted. Soon the tops of thousands of spiky plants were filled with golden fruit glowing in the sun.

The new cannery provided jobs for those who wanted to escape the onerous work of the sugar plantations. A few bold individuals left the fields and started service industries: dairy farms, slop collection for pigs, auto garages, and other small businesses. Land was affordable in Kapa'a. Hard working poor people could acquire it, build homes, open businesses, and raise families.

In our walk we passed the Filipino store, Yoshimura's Fish Market, Yaka's bakery, Rialto Theater where my dad showed motion pictures. Near it was Joe's Barber Shop and Tanaka's mercantile store. Kapa'a was a town with a kaleidoscope of multi-cultures living in it.

At the fence by my auntie's house, I stopped to chat with my cousin's Portuguese husband Joe Rodriguez, a school teacher. His wife, Helen, of Hawaiian-French-Irish extraction, was also a teacher.

As I talked with Rodriguez, Joe, the Hawaiian cop, passed by and I said, "Eh Mr. Kauhunale, can kids go to the Puerto Rican dance hall?"

The police officer frowned. "Bobby, don't let me catch you in that taxi dance place. I'll put you in jail." Then he added with a smile, "It costs a dime a dance. You don't have the money."

I wiggled my hands in the empty pockets of my shorts, shrugged, and said, "No money, but watching is free."

Prim, proper, and practical, Joe Rodriguez said, "Be a good boy and stay out of places that can get you in trouble."

I nodded, smiled, and pulled Ambrose aside whispering, "We can go to the cock fights at Pueo Camp. That's free."

"Yeah, but the cops raid that Filipino camp sometimes. We will get good licking if we are caught. Besides, I think the rooster fights are on Saturday afternoon or Sunday."

"Maybe, those guys work five or six days a week in the cane fields. Maybe they have time in the evening to have a fight."

"Don't think so. Pueo's run by the sugar plantation. Lots of regulations. Lights out by eight o'clock. Wake up at four-thirty in the morning. No time for gambling on work days."

"Well, maybe we can go over to the Chinese flop house and watch the rice workers suck on their hookah pipes. The water smoke is sweet and makes you feel good."

"Ma says those guys get goofy with smoking. They puff, lie down and have dreams. She says bad to smell the stuff. Better we play agates instead."

"Nah. How about the pool hall? My dad might be there."

"Good. I like cigar smoke. Great smell."

"And after that maybe we get saimin at Kinko's."

"No money."

"Filipinos like kids. Pete will take care of us."

"Kinko lady won't go for it."

"Maybe, but she's sweet on Pete. Besides, I slip him a ticket to the movies."

Ambrose whistled, "I thought your dad was tough on free tickets?"

"Yeah, on giving away anything for free he says that is how you 'go broke ass.' But my mom slips me free passes."

"Let's smell some smokes," Ambrose said.

"Click, clack." The sound repeated constantly as cue balls struck other round wooden balls that caromed off the rubber cushions. Four green felt tables had action going on each one as cue sticks smashed and a purple or red or orange ball plumped into the corner pockets and rolled into a hold- ing pen. A successful shooter would reach up with his cue stick and slide a bead across a wire.

In the dingy room, lit only by an overhead rack of three green shaded lamps, no one noticed two skinny kids sneaking in. "They puffing hard on cigars," Ambrose said. "Room is full of smoke like we in clouds."

"Scratch dis one," a man said as he grabbed a square of chalk and rubbed up his cue stick.

"Is that your dad over there?" Ambrose pointed to a man wearing a black toupee.

"No. My mother doesn't like him gambling. But he loves it. The guy with the dark wig is losing. See any beads on his side of the wire?"

Ambrose shook his head, "Not only losing, but losing big."

The wig howled as he scratched a shot. His opponent smirked, his finger crossing his throat. An older guy in a long sleeved shirt stepped in and began to rack the balls. Toupee fumed.

Ambrose said, "Trouble coming. I heard the guy say something like 'suk suk manouk'. Let's go."

"What do those Tagalog words mean?"

Ambrose smiled, "Having sex with a chicken."

"What's sex?"

"Stupid, sex is what produces babies."

"I thought the stork brought babies," I said, shaking my head. "Come on, let's eat."

At Kinko's, next to the pool hall, Pete scooped out noodles with a small fish net from a steaming pot. He cast an eye on us as we sidled onto the round stools fronting a long wood counter. There was only one other patron in the shop.

"Two small," I said, my voice wavering since neither of us had a penny. But I clutched insurance in my pocket.

Pete raised an eyebrow, filled two small bowls with noodles, flavored hot water, strips of pork, and cut onions. He brought the food to us.

"Why is your soup so good?" Ambrose asked.

"The pork bone. Use same bone every day. Save little bit of the soup each night for the next day. You like?"

"You're the best on the island," I said.

Pete beamed.

"Anything happening at Pueo?" This was the big Filipino camp on the west edge of Kapa'a town. The plantations had a habit of keeping their laborers separated by race and quartered in small enclosures by the sugar mill or near the cane fields. The idea is to keep the imported workers separated, each faction divided and easily ruled. That's why Kapa'a was unique, an integrated multi-racial town, where everybody struggled, but all worked together to help each other survive.

Pete looked for the pay.

I offered some free movies, taking rectangular green cardboard strips from my pocket.

Pete nodded.

"Anything going?" I asked again.

"I know nothing. But Sunday is a special day."

Did Pete mean a special church day or was there action at Pueo? I didn't know, but one thing was sure, I would try to get there after mass.

* * *

Foam-crowned waves smashed into the Kealia shore, rushed up its slope, spilling in a widening fan of bubbling water into the stagnant river. Its outlet to the sea was shuttered up with sand banked high by the mass of waves surging against the beach. Several yards from the water, beneath the berm of the railroad tracks girdling the shoreline, palm trees rustled in the stiff breeze.

A chorus sang *Kyrie Eleison* as a priest uttered the Jesus Prayer at Saint Catherine's Church on the hillside above Kealia beach. I fidgeted in my seat as I listened to the singers begging for the Lord's mercy. I couldn't fathom what they had done wrong. More to the point, I couldn't understand the liturgy said and sung in Latin.

My European grandfather fled the province of Alsace to avoid impressment into the Kaiser's army. He traveled until he arrived on Kaua'i, married, and made a home in Kapa'a. A good Catholic, he fathered twelve children and his family followed his faith. My Hawaiian-Portuguese dad was Catholic, but not devout. He had lived in the Philippines for a time and believed the Church took undue advantage of the poor people. My French-Hawaiian mother professed Catholicism but still dabbled in the paganism of the *kahuna*.

Much to my dislike, I had to practice all the rituals and try my best to be good. Otherwise the "body of Jesus," the communion wafer, would burn me. That was an unusual belief, but all part of religious mind control.

I had to pay attention to a service I couldn't understand and my thoughts wandered. What could be going on in Pueo camp? Something naughty. Hurry up, priest. Finish the service so I can get into trouble.

The heavenly father intoned, "Dominus Vobiscum." I knew we were plodding to the finish line when god's spokesman said, "The Lord be with you."

The choir returned his blessing from their perch on the second floor, "Et cum spiritu tu-oh." For years I thought they were saying, "Here comes spirit two-two-0." Later in life I learned that they were responding, "And with your spirit." A good answer, but why say it in Latin? We are taught in school to speak English, "the language of America." In church, we lived in a foreign land.

With a flourish the priest administered the final blessing. The organ pealed triumphant. The mass was over. I stood with the Portuguese families who formed the bulk of the town's Catholics. I took a covert glance at the half dozen icons perched on pedestals lining the hallway. The saints glowered. My belly tightened. My heart thumped. Did they know my intentions? My desire to see the dark side of life in Pueo evaporated. My eyes dropped to the checkered tile. Scuffing my feet on the black and white squares, I scurried past the adults and outside the door.

I glanced beyond the church to the graveyard. Rows of crosses sloped down the hill. In this hallowed ground none of my Hawaiian ancestors were buried. They were either in Protestant graveyards or asleep in the way of the old religion.

Once outside, courage returned. I hopped into the back of the family truck. My parents and sister sat in front. On the drive home I worked on an excuse to go to Kapa'a, "My Morgan cousins are going swimming at the beach."

My bold plan evaporated when my mother said, "You can't go with Ambrose. Trouble at their house last night. You go straight to the Morgans. Report to your Aunt Katie. Don't go by way of Waitala, ghosts will eat you up."

"Orders, orders, orders," I thought. "You can't do this. You can't do that. Nag, nag, nag." That's all moms do. Just wait until I'm grown up, then I'll do what I want. I didn't dare disobey, the licking would make my legs burn.

I marched up to Kapa'a with an escort, a maid. Rats. Morose, I went into Aunt Katie's house. Her two adult children had gone to the Rialto to work. It left two younger male cousins who did not want to be saddled with "the skinny kid." But Katie was adamant, "Take him to the beach."

Out the rear door we went. Railroad tracks paralleling the back road curved toward the hills. My two cousins followed it. "Hey," I called, "the beach is the other way."

"Shut your big mouth. Say nothing. Keep the secret."

Whoopee! They were heading for Pueo.

When we entered the walled compound containing a dozen or more hovels, the talk is all about the battles to come. Rooster fighting was not exciting. Most of it was show and tell. Betting on a winner was the most important part. Each owner parades his pet around, displaying his cock and the three-inch knife attached to each foot. As they stride about stroking their bird, they brag, "Dis one, one tough bugga. Give the knife. No can lose."

In the actual combats, the two roosters may be tethered so they can't run away. Sometimes they are let free to battle each other without restraints. These birds will posture, cluck, stretch their necks, cock an eye, and raise their hind feathers high. At some point a rooster will charge. One of two things happens, the opposing animal will attack and razor sharp knives slash and cut until death occurs, or a coward runs away screaming. That bird will steam in a pot that night.

But the combats aren't the fun of cock fighting. It's the stories the men tell, like the time when two factions bet hundreds of dollars on the result of a match. The rooster of one group slashed his opponent to death, the sand of the ring darkened with his spurting blood. The winning group demanded their money until a Chinese, built like a sumo wrestler, entered the combat circle and sliced off the neck of the winner saying, "It's a draw." No one argued with his decision.

There was other money action beside cock fighting, wagering on dice rolls and card games like Paiute, a Hawaiian poker game. And then there were the women.

Filipinos came to Hawai'i to work in the sugar fields without wives or families. They were lonely men who were kind to kids. On my visit to

Pueo, in a back alley hovel, two scantily dressed women entertained affection-starved men. At the time, I didn't understand what was happening. Today I realize how important it was for a man to have the scent and feel of a woman. Even though the pleasure she gives may be brief, the sensations were long and lasting. To quote the song from *South Pacific*, "There is nothing like a dame, nothing in the world."

CHAPTER 6

The Ocean

A volcanic island without resources, thousands of miles from any continent, with limited means of communication, was stifling. Add to it an agricultural economy subject to all of nature's misfortunes, serviced by a disparate population of imported races without a common language, and you have a recipe for poverty, class warfare, and anarchy.

Despite a Great Depression there did not occur a Darwinian battle for survival of the fittest. Instead, the polyglot races on the island of Kaua'i worked together, shared with each other in the Hawaiian way, and developed a common language, Pidgin.

Life in the 1930s was simple. With nothing to acquire, greed was absent, stress was non-existent. You made what you needed or traded for what you did not have. Accumulating money was not the purpose of existence.

There was a minimal realization among the multi-race population that they were the broad base of a sharply pointed pyramid. For the Hawaiian, this was acceptable. In ancient times there had existed a two-tiered society, the chiefs and priests at the highest level and the mass of commoners at the bottom.

In the plantation era, at the top perched two percent of the population. This was the elite class of wealthy rulers of the islands. Some of this group practiced plantation paternalism, a philanthropy that provided schools and hospitals for the common folk. But others among the privileged few created a racial dividing line. Prejudice against people of color, endemic in the southern United States, was replicated in Hawai'i.

Land is power. Realization of this fact resulted in the early colonizers pursuing land ownership. On Kaua'i in the 1930s, fifty percent of the land was controlled by ten owners and forty-four percent by the government. Land available to the commoners was not suitable for sugar cultivation. Kapa'a grew to be a free town because it was surrounded by water, marshland to the west and the ocean to the east. The plantations did not want it.

For many miles along the coast, sugar cane or pineapple fields covered the arable land from the mountains to the sea. Private farms were few in number since good acreage and available water were controlled by big business. This vice grip on land along the sea shore affected accessibility to the ocean. It meant either trespass over private property or hiking along the rocky shoreline to get to places where ocean products could be acquired.

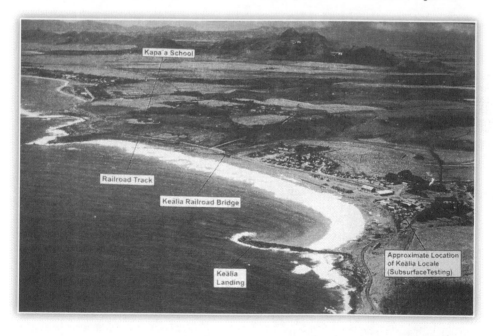

With real estate on the island controlled by a few, the only hope for sustainability by the many was access to the sea. The ocean provides a limitless playground for children. The ironing board served as my surfing vessel. But canoes that had once sailed between the islands were not available for children.

With the help of a kindly Filipino man, my friends and I fashioned a tin boat out of unwanted metal roofing. Using a two-by-four for a prow, a crescent-shaped piece of wood for a stern, we bent the metal into the shape of a boat. The pieces of wood were nailed to the curved tin and roofing tar used to seal cracks. Once done, we had a watertight tin canoe.

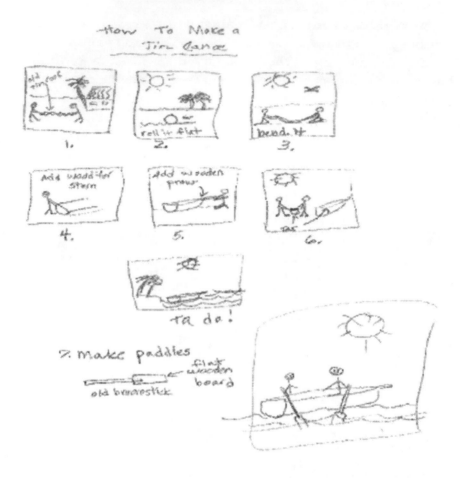

Though buoyant, the metal craft was tipsy. There was no centerboard to steady it from adverse wind or wave action. It requires perfect balance to keep the canoe from sinking. Unlike wooden crafts, once submerged, tin will not rise to the surface. We did not have a pond to practice in, only the ocean with its restless turbulence.

My best friend Sooky and I tried to accomplish the impossible, stay afloat. Entering the canoe was an ordeal, the waves unbalanced it. Sharp edges cut the skin. Each boy-sailor needed to enter from opposite sides of the vessel, and together. For an hour we tried and floundered. Our legs and arms were slashed by metal and blackened with roofing tar that oozed from the cracks in the fitted wood.

"Shall we quit?" I asked.

Sooky shook his head. Our canoe swept up the sand and, pulled by a wave, bobbed out to sea.

"Hey. Grab the boat," I yelled.

We splashed into the water as the current drew the craft toward the deep. Gulping ocean, we chased after it. A wave smashed the broadside of the canoe sinking it.

"Not going out to sea anymore," I muttered.

Sooky shivered, "How we get it up?"

The ocean's surge scraped the tin canoe along the coral bottom. "Maybe we let the waves push the thing in," I said.

"Boat will get broken."

"We lift it together. Roll it over." A simple solution, but a difficult maneuver to execute.

"We work together," I said as Sooky reached for the bow and I grasped the stern of the boat. My bare feet sought a purchase on the sharp coral. A wave pulled the stern from my hand and washed over Sooky, submerging him. Our boat scraped the bottom, bumping toward shore.

"Shallow," I yelled. "Touching sand."

These factors gave us a chance.

"Together, lift and turn."

We raised the metal boat, weightless while underwater.

"Roll it," I said as the upper edges of the tin canoe broke the surface.

We turned the boat over. Emptied the water and rolled it over again. It floated on the surface. Pulling the canoe back to land, we collapsed on the sand. "Want to quit?" I asked.

"No."

"Then we go again."

Several sinkings later we finally stayed afloat for several minutes. Now we faced the ultimate test, paddling out to sea into countless waves rushing toward the shore.

"We paddle together, you on the right, me on the left side. We keep a steady rhythm. Aim the front into the waves," I said.

Our boat crested the first two waves, the prow knifing like an arrow into the curving walls of water, bobbing over and down into the trough of each wave. But early success led to mistakes. We did not synch our paddling. The tin canoe turned broadside into a wave and *auwe huli*, we turned over and sank.

"Quick," said Sooky. "You're taller, grab the front and lift. I'll push from the back."

I grasped his idea, have the boat exit the water by angling the vessel upward. It would be difficult but doable. We dove together. I pulled up the front and the prow broke the surface. I kept lifting and Sooky pushed the bow out of the water.

The maneuver worked. Our boat bobbed on the surface, but how to get in? The edges of the hull were sharp and my feet could barely touch bottom.

We pushed the boat into shallow water. Once the sea stood waist high, we positioned ourselves on opposite sides of the tin canoe. I shouted the cadence, "one, two, and three together." We grasped the edges of the vessel. It wobbled. We paused, steadying the dancing craft, metal scoring the palms of our hands. I yelled, "Go." In one quick move, we crawled into the tipsy canoe.

"Grab the paddles and pull," I said as the wave action turned the boat broadside. But our earlier practice had taught us how to work together. We righted the tin canoe and pushed out to sea.

Our practice and experience paid off. We stroked in synch. Waves kept challenging us, tossing our boat up and down. With mighty efforts the ocean tried to sink our canoe seeking to end our day's efforts with the misery of having our metal craft plunged to the bottom.

We were up to the challenge. As a special reward, we accomplished the difficult feat of turning our boat, catching a wave, and surfing toward shore. We almost made it but the wave broke into foam, filling the hull with water.

Dragging the tin canoe across the sand, I thought of the lessons learned. Staying afloat in a tin canoe was like life, you are pushed up, down, and sideways. But if you work together keeping the boat steady and on course you can make it to your final destination.

* * *

Ancient Hawaiians survived by harvesting from the sea. They passed on their knowledge to succeeding generations. *Opihi*, a limpet poisonous in California, is a highly desirable food in Hawai'i, especially when garnished with *limu*. This is a seaweed scraped from the reef. Some people call it Pele's hair, for its color is red like burning lava.

The fire goddess lives in the heart of Kilauea volcano, a steaming and unpredictable caldera spewing molten rock over the countryside. According to legend Pele does not remain in her hot home. Beware if you are driving late at night and happen upon an old woman. Give her a ride or else big *pilikia* (trouble).

To scrape *limu* from the reef our family left early in the morning when the horizon turned pink. Plantation fields and fences blocked our entry to the gathering place. We were forced to take a circuitous route through Hawaiian homesteads to get to the beach.

At the shore, brown reefs thrust above the water as the ocean receded from the shoreline. "Go quick," said cousin Pono, pointing to black rocks. "Tide will come back soon." Four of us hurried onto the round stones, and like crabs we used our hands and feet to scurry along the boulders.

"Look at the *opihi*," Stan said. Like a monkey, he scampered to pink rocks swept over by a surging sea. He began prying from the stones large pyramid-shaped limpets.

"We can't stop," said Aunt Katie. "Come."

Stan continued harvesting. He loved scraping *opihi* from the rocks. He loved challenging the sea.

"Wave coming," shouted Pono.

I saw by the intensity in his eyes that Stan had fixed upon a grandfather-sized *opihi*, its top sprouting a forest of seaweed. His knife slipped between rock and shell and he started the twist that loosens the limpet from the stone. The wave hit, shoving him into rocks and receded, drawing him toward deeper water.

Fortunately the ocean did not have a heavy surge. Stan fought his way out of the sea and scrambled up the boulders.

"*Hele mai lolo* (Come, you foolish one)," said Aunt Katie.

A chastised Stan followed us. I didn't say a word. He is bigger and I might be cuffed for foolish prattle.

"Be seen but not heard. Speak when you are spoken to." These are the maxims of the Morgan family. Swift is the enforcement of these basic principles, a sound thrashing of the buttocks and legs. But the Morgans who were with me this day were not the punishers. The Tsar of terror was the oldest, Albert. Despite his absence, I kept my peace.

We climbed a knoll of boulders. Near the top, a fresh wind ruffled my hair, dried my t-shirt, and whipped the legs of my khaki shorts. Scrambling upon a large round rock I stood amazed. A small bay lay below. A shelf of calcified stone spread out into the sea. Along its edges flowing into emerald green water were long strands of iodine-colored seaweed. Pele's hair waved like shredded red flags in the undulating water. It was an awesome sight.

Our group hurried onto the reef, its surface wet, mossy, and slick. The coral-crusted lava shelf was pocked with holes and rifts. Peering into crevices, I saw really big fish. They challenged me. Rising from deep caverns, the saucy animals stared with unblinking eyes into mine. After a moment of taunting, they peeled into slits in the rock. Their insouciance roused a desire to leap in and catch them. But fear of what lurked within the stone, a lack of equipment, and the necessity of scraping the *limu* before the tide came in halted my dive. "Someday," I vowed, "I will go under water and capture you."

Like shearing sheep, I used a sharp scissors to separate the seaweed from the coral rock. I had been taught to avoid breaking the stone from which the *limu* grows. The stubs of roots will grow again.

The greatest danger in harvesting comes from a swelling sea. A rogue wave can sweep you from the shelf and pull you into the ocean.

"You stay back," said Aunt Katie, pointing to the emerald green of the deep beyond the ledge.

"Always picking on me," I muttered. In a louder voice I said, "Why?"

"Look around. All rocks. Ocean grabs you then *maki* (die)."

Despite my annoyance, I could see she had a point. There was no friendly sand beach to swim to. To escape from the ocean I would have to clamber over rocks. Still, I pouted. I could swim. I could overcome the sea. If my ancestors feared the ocean, they would never have traveled the thousands of miles to find Hawai'i.

But obedience to elders was ingrained and enforced by the flat side of a stick. My uttered "why" was insubordination. But my aunt was tolerant. I complained no more and hung back from the rest of the pickers, content to gather the smaller tufts of seaweed while the older family members worked near the edge of the reef harvesting *limu*.

Living by the sea, I respected its power. But whether I was too young or too inexperienced to know better, I did not let fear cripple my curiosity. For at the seashore and beneath the surface were good things to eat, wonders to see, and adventures to be enjoyed.

* * *

Bristling with sharp pointed spines, *wana*, a sea-urchin, appears to be the last edible in the food chain. Treacherous are their waving purple spear points. Needle sharp, a poke into the skin by one of the creature's spikes can result in a devastating infection. I have seen more than one moray eel bristling with the dangerous quills in its snout. It's a deadly price to pay for the succulent purple morsel hidden within the hard shell of the animal.

Wana clusters within crevices in the reefs. Why they enjoy being grouped together, I do not know, but beware of stumbling into one of these forests of sea porcupines when the tide is rolling in. The crashing water covers the purple horde in foam, any movement risks stepping into a host of underwater spears.

You might say, "Stay clear of the critters. What good are they?"

But eels know something about what tasty edibles are protected by sheaves of needles, and so did the ancient Hawaiians. When people were starving, they turned to the ugly *wana* for food.

I never had a hankering for the purple tongue-shaped urchins nestled in a shell surrounded by spears, but older folk loved them. How they were captured in olden times was beyond my knowledge. But on the day I learned to harvest them, I used a malleable length of metal fashioned into a two-pronged rake.

It was low tide with the surface of the reefs free of foam. I approached the forests of *wana* carefully. The urchins sensed my coming. Their sharp spines swiveled in my direction like needles attracted by a magnet. I was the polarizing point. When I came to the first creature, its sharp spears waved rapidly, then stiffened. They stood poised like arrows ready to fly into my eyes. For a moment I felt like a pin cushion threatened by scores of sharp needles.

Fear paralyzed me. Nature's protection of its purple creatures held me rigid, uncertain as to what to do.

"No be scared," said Jack, an experienced fisherman and friend of the family. "Reach your rake behind it. Then pull toward you and up."

Simple advice, but water is a refracting prism that bends light. Standing above the surface, my attempt went awry and I scraped reef, missing the body of the creature. Its spines waved in derision, taunting me for my ineptness. I shook my head, disgusted with my failure. The *wana* does not move. But its psychological protections of sharp waving points frightened me and made my hand shake when I tried to unfasten the creature from the rocks.

Jack shook his head and moved his hand with a raking motion.

"I'm afraid. What if it spears my body? Its poison might kill me."

Jack laughed. "No worry. I pee on it. Kill the poison. Make the spear come out."

"You try."

Jack shook his head. "Take your time. *Wana* can't run away."

That put a new slant on things. I certainly could capture an unmoving object. Reaching with my rake I prepared to plunge it beyond the spines and pull in the baseball-sized object made huge by its quills. As I started my move a wave washed over my target, spoiled my vision, and I scraped coral.

Failure made me want to swear, but for Catholics it would mean severe penance, at least ten Our Fathers and Hail Marys. I curbed my curse. I looked at Jack for instruction. He put his hand into the water, extending it out to the fearsome critter. "Take your time. Watch the waves. When ready, pull."

I could see he had a hooped net to capture the animal once freed from the rock. His certainty that I would succeed gave me courage. I watched the wave action, waited for the foam to clear. A lull in the turbulence of the water came. I thrust my rake past the horrid spines, anchored it behind the animal, twisted and pulled the *wana* from the rocks.

Jack scooped up the creature before it tumbled away with the current. "Good job," he said.

I had made my first *wana* capture. Oh, what joy to be a successful ocean predator. It may not seem like much, but it beats cutting seaweed and unmoving limpets, for only a turbulent ocean protects them. But the purple ocean porcupine has stingers that can be deadly. This is the thrill of taking *wana*, overcoming fear and being praised for your bravery.

* * *

Dark brown and banana shaped, the *loli* looks like an object commonly flushed out of sight. Ugly and slippery to the touch, I could not believe that anyone would want it. But Asian friends rave about sea cucumber soup, the finest of any that is made.

Ancient Hawaiians did not eat it. It was given as a gift of undying love. They claimed it has aphrodisiac qualities. They also used it for medicine.

I do not know the truth of either claim. All I will say about the creature is that it is flexible like rubber, crawls slowly on the sea bottom using tube feet to move, and eats sand for food. Diving for fish, I would watch a *loli* leave a trail of disgorged white sand flowing behind it as it wound its way along the reef. Snatching the creature from the rocks I would find its slippery body coated on its underside with sticky sand. Why?

Nature had provided the creature with a unique defense mechanism. It spills its guts. When I grasped a *loli* it would vomit a disgusting string of white sticky intestines that coated my hand and body with a slime which fastened onto my flesh like glue. It is akin to walking into a spider's web underwater. I could not get rid of the cloying loathsome white strings.

One other piece of information, *loli* improperly cleaned and cooked can be poisonous.

Why do I mention the *loli* at all? Simply this, ancient Hawaiians would have starved if they did not use all the resources available to them. Imagine for a moment, landing upon a beautiful island that did not have anything to eat. These early explorers brought with them sprouts to be planted and pigs to be eventually eaten. But it takes a year for taro to reach maturity. It takes time for a sow to produce piglets and then more piglets. There are natural disasters to contend with that can destroy what you are trying to grow. Starvation is a grim reaper that is always at the side of a pioneer.

But if you understand the ocean and what it provides, you will not starve. For many of the Hawaiian people whom I grew up with, access to the sea was essential. From it they gathered *limu* for vitamins and used it as a garnish, *opihi* and *wana* for meat, and the *loli* for medicine. Growing up in Hawai'i the greatest threat to the Hawaiian people were the plantation fences with their "keep out" signs that prevented access to the sea.

CHAPTER 7

Sorcerers And Shamans

Magical characters and twilight blood suckers dominate our media. What is paranormal is the stuff that produces vast audiences of worshipers who make the deliverers of these macabre fantasies billionaires.

For centuries, religion has suppressed the worship of the occult and the practitioners of necromancy. Such pursuits are considered Satanic and a denial of the existence of God, the all powerful. But over these many hundreds of years, magical beliefs and practices persist in civilized societies and can be more interesting than the wonders of advancing technology.

When the Calvinist missionaries came to Hawai'i, they did not find idols to gods, for these had been thrown down months before their arrival. What they found were professionals called *kahuna*. Some of them, the *ana ana*, could pray you to death.

"Blasphemy," said the preachers from the pulpits. This castigation by civilized white men of pagan beliefs led to suppression of the *kahuna*. Their profession was made illegal in Hawai'i.

In reality the majority of *kahuna* are not shamans practicing dark arts, they are experts in medicine, fishing, building, and many other categories of special knowledge that allows a society to prosper. Only a few were of the *ana ana* persuasion that used psychological ploys to put the superstitious to death.

Despite the efforts of the *haole* to suppress the *kahuna*, they did not disappear. Instead, they escaped into the hills and continued to use their special knowledge. With their survival, the ancient belief systems in the spirits and the *aumakua* persisted. This was especially true on Kaua'i. Who can blame the Hawaiians of my home island for persisting in their reliance on the *kahuna*? It was they who uttered a *puleleileho ka moana* and raised a huge storm that destroyed Kamehameha's invasion fleet in 1796.

Again in 1804 the ruler of the islands recruited a mighty army. Human sacrifices were given to the war god Ku. Consulting the auguries, the high priest promised a successful conquest of Kaua'i.

Across the seventy-mile stretch of water the *ana ana* of the isolated island uttered *pule o'o,* prayers of extinction against the vast forces of the great king. A mighty host of warriors assembled on the beach at Waikiki ready to launch the invasion. The *mai akua* struck. This illness of the gods, typhoid fever, turned men black and thousands died.

With these defeats of Kamehameha the Great, the power of the *kahuna* became ingrained in the psyche of the common Hawaiian. Despite the efforts of Protestants and Catholics, those of half-blood, like the elders of my family raised by Hawaiian grandparents, clung to the old belief system. It is easy to scoff at these uncivilized convictions, but if you have experienced the unexplainable, like I have, then you might accept that the power of the *kahuna* is more than psychological.

My mother and aunts certainly believed. The men in the family were reluctant to acknowledge the superstitious claims as true, but they did not have the courage to contradict shamanistic practices. Some examples follow.

Aumakua means a deified ancestor that is a family or personal god. Such a deity could be a shark (*mano*), owl (*pueo*), or even a rock. It is believed that the possessor of the *aumakua* can summon it for assistance. My mother and several of my aunts swear that our Hawaiian grandfather could call the shark to aid him in fishing. In hushed voices they whispered of grandpa's *aumakua,* his *mano* who swam between his legs and chased fish into his net.

In low tones, my mother related stories of living in Ko'olau, a primitive, spooky place. At the time of the death of a relative, the *kahuna* would come. Mysterious words were uttered over the corpse. What other rituals were practiced she never said. But sometime during the night a whistling sound rose from the dead. The whistling left the shack, whirled outside and eventually faded away. What form this released spirit might take, she never explained other than to say "it can be controlled by your grandfather."

A cock-and-bull story, you say. Then speak to my friend Sooky. His cousin was possessed by the spirit of her dead four-year-old sister. The poltergeist-type events were witnessed by thousands on Kaua'i. In my own experience Gladys, a female friend of my mother and father, visited from San Francisco. The family toured the island and near the end of the trip they explored the caves of Ha'ena. That night Gladys fell seriously ill. The neighborhood doctor could not diagnose her ailment. It was suggested that she be moved to a room with more light and air. Miraculously, her condition improved and she was able to leave the island to return home.

But my father, who had changed rooms with her, fell ill. The doctor could not cure him. His fever rose so high that the priest was called to administer the last rites. My mother and aunts were suspicious. They checked under his bed and found rocks that Gladys had picked up from a cave in Ha'ena. Remember that *akua* can take the shape of a rock, and caves in olden times were used as burial places. Gladys had been admonished not to pick up stones at the sites she visited, but she had not heeded this warning.

Quick as a wink mother drove to Ha'ena. She took the rocks back to the cave that had been despoiled. Returning home, my father's fever broke and he was fine the next day.

All of what transpired can be logically explained. But none of my family will disturb rocks from a cave and I suggest, if you visit the caves of Kaua'i, that you leave the rocks alone.

There was a belief that if coldness grips your toes in the night and the icy chill works up your legs into your upper body, that an *ana ana* was praying you to death. I have not experienced coldness, but a *kahuna* aided me in warding off evil from an enemy. Of course when you are eight years old and you are told an enemy is causing you illness, you're susceptible to giving credence to the claim. Just like at Boy Scout camp when you are taken at night to catch snipe.

There are specialists who delve in the psychic world. From this source they can identify enemies that are using occult powers to cause you *pilikia,* trouble. These sorcerers can summon spirits they control to counteract the

evil perpetrated upon you. All this my mother explained as she dragged me
into the audience room of an aged seer.

Chambers, dark like a witch's cave, enveloped me. Shivering I peered
about the fearsome place expecting skulls and bones like in the movie,
Treasure Island. In the shadows two feathered *kahili*, a sign of royalty, thrust
upward to the ceiling. Shuddering, I stood frozen in place until my mother
patted my behind and pushed me toward an old crone seated in a wicker
chair the size of a throne.

Black clothes covered her from neck to toes. Strands of salt and pepper hair draped over her shoulders, falling past ample breasts and resting on a protruding tummy. It was difficult to gauge her height since her
chair rested on a raised platform, but it was obvious she was corpulent and
ancient.

The cause of my coming was asthma. It had hit me like a thunder bolt
and sickened me to the point that I could not be active. Effort caused
coughing that sometimes became uncontrollable. My superstitious mother
knew I had an enemy and ushered me to the *kahuna*. As she pushed me
toward the old woman, she said, "Tell your dream."

Crackling, like static electricity, buzzed the air. Luminous eyes peered
at me. I fidgeted, hopping back and forth, finally balancing on one leg,
rubbing my foot against it. With my throat dry, I couldn't utter a sound.

"Wa'la au (speak)," said the *kahuna*.

It was easy for her to say, but hard to do. *Kahunas* have magical powers
that can shrivel your body or snatch your soul. At least that was what the
elders in the family had explained to me. Standing before the woman I felt
like the tin man facing the mighty wizard of Oz. Mother came to my aid,
and told my dream of a Frankenstein-sized monster pursuing me.

I found my voice and said, "Big guy. Green face. Very ugly." I explained
his attempts to catch me and then stopped talking.

"Au'we (too bad)," the *kahuna* lady said, then motioned my mother to
her side and they spoke in Hawaiian. Exactly what transpired I do not
know for certain, but I understood enough to know that my family had an
enemy, a name was mentioned, and the old woman promised to exercise her
magical powers to counteract the evil attacks being perpetrated upon me.
At the end of the conversation I saw green bills being transmitted from my
mother to the *kahuna*.

On my way home, Mom admonished me not to let any of my personal items like fingernails or strands of hair be placed into the garbage. "Bury them in secret," she said.

Despite all precautions and the *kahuna's* intercession, my asthma did not vanish until much later in my life. I never understood why we prayed for God's help on Sunday and on Monday paid the kahuna to use magic powers to aid me. But for people like my mother, who was half Hawaiian and raised in the old ways, what she did made sense. Cover all the bases by placating all supreme beings.

But the most frightening spooks of all are the night marchers, dead chiefs and warriors intent on fighting old battles or seeking their way to the next world. The lore has it that they march to the sound of the *pahu* drums, chanting *oli* as they stride. You dare not interrupt their wandering. "Crouch low. Play dead," was the advice of the elders. "Do not look in their eyes or you will be snatched up and march with them into hell."

Falderal and balderdash you say, but there have been many a late night driver traveling the highway between the county jail and Lihue that have blamed their car crash on the night marchers. Others will swear they have heard the strident steps and rhythmic chanting of the ghosts in the early morning before the cock crows.

An isolated island surrounded by a crashing sea and buffeted by winds rattling windows, shaking trees, creating weird noises. Sudden darkness as soon as the sun sets with only faint lantern light to part the gloom. These are the ingredients that produce a mental cauldron of superstition. Christianity has been in the islands for a century. Religious efforts to suppress the *kahuna* only produced a stubborn clinging to the old beliefs.

Fascination with the occult and other world phenomenon has survived through the ages. Why? There are unusual events that defy logical explanations. As an example on the Big Island, there are stories of Pele's lava being diverted by *kahuna* intervention. There are other tales of strange happenings in Hawai'i without any other explanation than magic.

It was wise for me not to oppose ancient beliefs. Who knows what evil might have occurred if the kahuna's power was challenged?

CHAPTER 8

In Search Of Santa Claus

"Twas the night before Christmas, and all through the house not a creature was stirring, not even a mouse." I recited the poem to thunderous applause by uncles and aunts in the common room of Grandpa's house. The rhyme spoke of stockings, chimneys, snow, extreme cold, reindeer, a sleigh, and a jolly old elf dressed in red fur that brought presents on Christmas Eve.

But though I was rewarded for my brilliant speech I knew nothing of what I recited that Xmas day. Without a chimney it was puzzlement as to how Santa Claus had delivered his presents. Snow is unknown on Kaua'i.

In my thin cotton shirt, I pondered what fur was and marveled that St. Nick in doing his gift giving was not drenched in sweat. But these are questions I did not dwell upon since I believed he existed. It was like the story of the stork bringing babies: I believed it to be true.

A few days after Christmas, I spoke with my best friend Sooky about the mysteries surrounding Santa Claus. "No chimney in the house, how does he get in?" I asked.

"Nobody locks the doors, he walks in."

"How does he come to the house?"

"Fly."

"How?"

"Skyrockets."

"Story says reindeer."

"No reindeer here. Santa Claus uses skyrockets."

I shook my head since nothing made sense.

"Let's ask him?" said Sooky.

"Where is he?"

Sooky pointed at Sleeping Giant Mountain three miles away. "He must live up there."

That made sense, for it was the tallest mound we could see. Most of the other mountains on the island were buried in clouds.

Barefoot, in shorts and t-shirts we headed off. We did not tell our mothers, since they would say no. But Sooky and I had a burning desire to find Santa Claus, get some toys, and learn how he did his magic in one night.

We scooted across the government road and found a path leading towards the cane fields and the Sleeping Giant. If you come to Kaua'i and travel to Kapa'a, you will see this mountain's face and squat body lying rigid, his right eye staring at the heavens. The legend is that centuries ago, the monster came ashore. He threatened to devour the people, but relented when they promised to bring him all the food he could eat. The elders soon realized that the giant would consume everything on the island including the people. They concocted a potent brew and offered it to the huge man. The beverage did the trick. The giant yawned, rolled onto his back, and went to sleep forever.

The pathway petered out near a ditch where the cane fields rose three times our height. A horse stood in a corral nearby.

"Ask him," Sooky said pointing to the animal.

Not a bad idea, I thought. Horses know a lot of things. I hitched up my pants, scuffed my feet in the dirt, and sidled up to the fence post. In an eager voice I said, "Horsey, do you know the way to Santa Claus?"

His tail flicked back and forth like a metronome. I knew he was thinking on the question because his unblinking eyes studied me very closely.

"He didn't hear you," Sooky said. "Where's Santa Claus?"

The horse snorted and moved away.

"Hey, he was about to tell me."

Sooky one-upped me, "Hay is for horses."

"We're not in school," I said and decided to aggravate him. "Hey, hey, I hear ducks."

Sooky waved a finger. "That's stupid."

"Just as stupid as talking to a horse."

I didn't wait for his response. I followed the slow moving stream heading off in the direction of the "quack, quacks."

White feathered footballs swam in a pond fed by water from the ditch. Their orange bills ducked beneath the surface, stirring up mud.

I figured there had to be a Chinese caretaker nearby. The *Pake* (elder uncle) raised ducks for food. Peking duck is out of this world good. Glazed with syrup until golden brown, they have a sweet flavor that classifies them as one of the world's top dishes. But stink duck eggs is another story. It was claimed that they taste best when cured over one thousand years. I don't know the truth, but my mother soaked eggs in brine for months, until they turned a sickly grey green. She sold or traded them to Asians who loved stink eggs. I did not like them. Their color and smell was putrid and made my stomach rumble.

I hustled to the edge of the pond, almost slipping in. That would have been a disaster since the bank was steep and I had not yet learned to swim. Sooky came up behind me calling, "How do we find Santa Claus?"

Like a fleet of sailing ships the covey of ducks headed for a reed-filled bank and waddled in.

"They know where," I said, sounding optimistic.

"We catch one. Ask him," Sooky said.

But our kidnap plans went awry when an old Chinese with a conical straw hat showed up.

"Eh *oleloa,* (worthless), what you want?"

This was a crucial moment: do we stand our ground and answer or run away? I looked at Sooky. He fidgeted. But we were on a mission and I did not intend to be sidetracked. Besides, the Chinese walked slow and I knew we could get away. Gulping air, I finally stammered, "Looking for Santa Claus."

"What that? Something to eat?"

"He brings presents at Christmas."

"Know nothing. Maybe you come steal duck?" said the Chinese, eyeing us with suspicion.

"You keep da kine ducks. No like," I said, denying any intent to steal. "We go Sleeping Giant. Find Santa Claus."

"Can you show the way?" Sooky interrupted.

"You cross ditch there," said the Chinese pointing, "path through cane fields. Other end near *No No* (Hawaiian name for Sleeping Giant Mountain, it means to snore). Watch out, fire cane pretty soon."

With a wave of his stick the *Pake* dismissed us and we trotted across the bridge and stomped onto a path kicking up clouds of dust as we ran along the ground. The slim pathway was bordered by stalks of cane. There had been no rain for awhile and the leaves were dried brown.

"Fire cane," the words echoed in my ears. I had seen plantation men spray the fields with kerosene, then set fire to the leaves. The flames spread fast, especially when the leaves were dry. I looked at the walls of stalks. "We're trapped," I said.

"I got to pee," Sooky answered.

"Scaredy cat." But suddenly I felt an overwhelming panic and an urge to go. I unbuttoned my shorts and let it flow.

From somewhere nearby I heard the rattle of a truck. It sounded like kerosene spray falling on leaves.

"Fire coming," I blurted. "Run."

But where? We had wandered into the thick of a jungle of cane stalks. I felt my body getting warmer, and I thought the burning had begun.

"Go this way," said Sooky, pointing toward the noise.

"No. Fire starts from there."

But my friend did not heed the warning and he disappeared into the leaves. What to do? Follow him and be roasted or retreat?

I made up my mind. Whatever happened, we would go together. "Sooky. Wait for me." With my heart in my throat, I plunged after him, the sound of his crashing through the leaves diminishing in my ears.

"Where are you?" I called, a panic setting in. Again I heard the sounds of spray falling on the leaves. I knew it would just be moments before the fires were lit. Never in my young life had I been so scared. Blazing heat flooded through the leaves. Golden light blinded my eyes. This is the end, I thought, roasted like a Peking duck.

"Over here," yelled Sooky.

I plunged toward his voice and stumbled through the stalks onto a plantation dirt road. The blazing noonday sun baked my scratched body. Nearby rumbled a truck with a tank resting on its bed, spraying the fields. A *luna* (supervisor) wearing denim blues with black boots covering his legs sat astride a horse watching.

"Hey, you kids. What you doing here? Go home."

I almost retorted "hay is for horses" but I knew that would cause trouble. Meekly, I asked, "Where go?"

The supervisor turned his horse and trotted to us. "What are you doing here? This is plantation property."

"Looking for Santa Claus," we said, adding, "He lives on *No No* Mountain."

"Santa Claus is not on that mountain. He is far away in the North Pole."

The *luna's* answer was devastating. We followed his directions to the government road and went home. Two worried mothers were waiting with long sticks. They whacked us hard until we promised not to wander off again. But despite the licking, I made plans to find the North Pole.

CHAPTER 9

My Town

Kapa'a means "the solid," a strange name for a piece of land surrounded by water. The Pacific lies to its east, marshland to the west, with two sluggish streams bisecting its one-mile length. In the past, when heavy rains came the town would be submerged. The soil is considered low-yielding, hence the plantations did not want it. There is little evidence of ancients living in Kapa'a. Most of the artifacts and monuments are found to the south, near the Wailua River. Despite its shortcomings, it is a unique town. It is a place that attracted poor people to acquire land, build homes, and raise families.

History is the story of people and events that got us where we are today. We need to delve into history to understand the uniqueness of my town. The Great Mahele (Division) of 1848 ended the communal use of Hawaii's land by its people and instituted private property ownership. This resulted in a sugar economy where a few controlled the arable land and displaced Hawaiians from it.

With a native population decimated by disease, the plantations fostered immigration laws which allowed for the importation of foreign workers. Thousands of multi-national contract laborers were brought in to work the fields.

When the Civil War shut down the sugar industry in the South, the United States became the biggest consumer of Hawaiian-grown sugar. To make huge profits, the plantation owners needed a reciprocity treaty with America. They caused to be elected king David Kalakaua, who promptly concluded a treaty in 1876. This ensured that Hawaiian grown sugar would be imported into America duty free. This opportunity to acquire wealth increased the seizure of arable land by plantation owners, spurred immigration, and wedded the fate of the Hawaiian nation to America.

All the usable land was not taken by the business interests. The *Mahele* set aside parcels of land for government use. One of those parcels was located in the area of Kapa'a.

After his successful conclusion of the Reciprocity Treaty, Kalakaua came to Kaua'i with a *Hui* (group) of his choral singers to take advantage of land he controlled. He and his followers built shanties and a sugar mill. At the same time, an enterprising Chinese acquired land in Kapa'a and planted rice.

Kalakaua's sugar enterprise failed. Singers are not sugar planters, but the rice farmer succeeded. He attracted other Chinese to the area and a small number of former plantation laborers and immigrants developed a community. When I grew up in Kapa'a, most of the merchants were Chinese.

The real growth of the town came after Hawai'i became a Territory of the United States. In 1907, the government subdivided land and sold it at prices poor people could afford. In that year the pineapple industry started on Kaua'i in Lawai. Six years later a pineapple cannery opened in Kapa'a and the rice community morphed into a fruit packing town.

Immigrant plantation workers left field work and took jobs at the cannery or began service industries. Wanderers from foreign lands and poor Hawaiians chose Kapa'a as a place to live, for land could be acquired cheaply. The sum of all this was a multi-cultural community whose people lived in freedom. Their lives were not controlled by the plantation owners. Kapa'a became a unique melting pot of many races where a polyglot of people lived together in peace.

In Kapa'a, during my growing up years, lived more than twenty ethnic groups: Chinese, Japanese, Okinawans, Portuguese, Spaniards, Americans, Puerto Ricans, French, Germans, Filipinos, Scots, Koreans, Poles, Swedes, just to name a few. Each grouping might be further divided by their dialect, culture, or religion.

There have been violent clashes between races and tribes throughout history. In Kapa'a you never called an immigrant from Okinawa, "Japanese." Japan in 1607 had overrun the Okinawan kingdom and imposed brutal martial law for nearly three hundred years.

For centuries, Hakka and Punti clans occupied the same province in China. In the mid- 19th century deadly internecine warfare killed millions. It was this area of China where labor recruiters from Hawai'i found workers for the sugar fields.

Filipinos came from three different areas of the Philippines: they were Ilocano's, Tagalogs, and Visayan. Each spoke a different language. They were not friendly with each other or with Americans who had suppressed Philippine insurgents with extreme cruelty.

In the labor massacre of 1924, Visayan strikers at a headquarters in Hanapepe seized Ilocano strike breakers. The rescue attempt of the kidnapped men by the sheriff resulted in sixteen deaths and many injuries. It is interesting to note that the Visayan chose Hanapepe and Kapa'a town to establish their strike bases. Why? They were the only two towns on the island not controlled by the sugar plantations. Incidentally, the sugar plantation owners determined to suppress the strike and supplied forty riflemen to the sheriff. These gunmen sworn in as deputy sheriffs caused the massacre.

For centuries, religious differences have divided people and led to warfare. There is no common religion in Hawai'i holding together the immigrant population. It is a mix of Catholics, Lutherans, Calvinists, Buddhists, Shinto worshipers, and other religious sects.

With this tinderbox of animosities you could expect racial strife and violence to explode in Kapa'a. It did not. Why not?

First, the immigrants and Hawaiians developed a common language, Pidgin. It allowed foreigners to communicate and learn the Hawaiian way, a communal sharing lifestyle filled with aloha. These values were adopted and practiced by all the immigrants who made Kapa'a their home.

As an example, my French grandfather fled his homeland, Alsace-Lorraine. The Germans had defeated the French in 1870, seized his province, and introduced the draft. He would not fight against his country. He ran as far as he could from the Kaiser and arrived on Kaua'i to become a plantation *luna*.

German Lutherans were contracted to work on Kaua'i. They were considered troublemakers by plantation management. Grandfather, who spoke their language, met with the unhappy people and learned that their *pilikia* stemmed from being unable to practice Lutheranism. His Hawaiian family provided a meeting hall for church services and, being a master chef, Grandfather cooked German meals for them.

My mother would always give gifts of food to poor families. Many times I delivered eggs, papayas, bananas, chickens, and other products to those in need. She made it a point to patronize everyone's shop, whatever the race. We did not have much, but we practiced *kokua* (helping others). That is the Hawaiian way, giving without expecting a reward.

Haven Kuboyama, long-time Kapa'a merchant, expressed the reason why Kapa'a was free of racial strife. "In the old days, no matter the nationality, we were all struggling to survive. Everybody helped each other. It was the good days."

Contrast this with a plantation community. The mill owners kept bringing in diverse races to tend the fields. They housed them in separate ethnic camps. They created a hierarchical caste system: white managers, field *lunas*, and laborers. They regulated work and living conditions. Laborers purchased necessities from the company store. The cost was deducted from their pay.

Why the importation of different races and ethnic separation? To prevent labor organization, demands for higher pay, and better working conditions.

These facts of life in Hawai'i before World War II explain the uniqueness of Kapa'a, a town where you escaped plantation oppression and lived in confined freedom in our small ghetto. Thousands of acres all around Kapa'a were controlled by the plantations and the ruling elite. Those of color could not enter their land without permission.

But in this small sphere of freedom we mixed well with each other. As a child I could lunch at a Chinese home on cha siu pork, soak in a steaming hot tub of the Japanese gardener in the evening, and receive malasadas from a Portuguese lady in the morning. For fun, a Filipino handyman gave me a bike and helped make a tin canoe, an Okinawan shopkeeper made me a metal spear.

There was a time when Kapa'a was barren with scattered grass shacks and taro patches. Sugar mills denuded the area of firewood. Chinese came and planted rice in the marshland. A small community of merchants and planters sprung up in the solid ground between the swamps and the sea.

Winds of change blew when the Hawaiian Pineapple Company built a cannery adjacent to Waikea Stream a year prior to the "Great War." Ten years later a devastating fire eliminated the aged buildings and a re-planning of the town followed. A residential sub-division was built south of Waikea, to serve as a middle-class suburb for Kapa'a. In the town, streets were laid out, fire protection rules enforced, and a general plan resulted in a well-ordered community.

In the 1930s, Kapa'a was a cannery town with a railroad track girdling the shoreline to transport pineapple to and from the packing plant. The shops and homes bordering the government highway were neat and well maintained with a minimum of signage. Homes reflected the nationalities living there. The Japanese had bonsai trees, the Chinese hung red lanterns on their porches with a little altar where incense or punk was burned to ward off evil spirits.

Kapa'a was different from a plantation community where everything centered on the mill and its plantation store. Single workers lived in walled, segregated camps and married men in small company shacks painted dark green, trimmed in white, with a tin roof and porch. Since the making of molasses was year-round, soot and sickly sweet smells pervaded the air.

Sugar cane processing requires huge resources of burning material, a ton of water to produce one pound of sugar, and the after-milling waste products results in mountains of trash. The plantations concentrated on importing a racially diverse work force to prevent strikes and keep labor costs to a minimum. This meant strict rules and regulations to keep workers in line and often harsh treatment like the Hanapepe massacre.

Contrast this with pineapple production in Kapa'a. Water usage was minimal, canning the fruit did not require excessive use of fossil fuels, there were sweet smells during the summer season but the town was not riven by the smoke and smells of burnt fibers from a belching plantation smokestack. Contract laborers did not compose the work force. Employment was by choice and not by seductive propaganda to con poverty-stricken foreign men into signing labor contracts. Unlike the plantations, management of Pono Cannery was worker-friendly and community oriented.

This is not meant as a castigation of plantations. Without sugar, Hawai'i would not have had an economy, a work force, and a means for Hawaiians to survive through inter-marriage. What I am saying is, if you started life in isolation and at the bottom of a society's sharp-pointed pyramid, then you were lucky to be born in Kapa'a.

CHAPTER 10

The Blessings Of Asthma

"I'll give him a shot to put him to sleep," Doctor Hata said. Even though I hated the sting of the needle, sleep was a blessing for the racking cough and wheeze had kept me awake for most of the night. I lay in my bed drenched in sweat, wishing I would die.

What had been carefree growing-up years turned into a nightmare. I could not be active without coughing. An attack forced me into my bed until the asthma subsided. I missed months of school and asthma obliterated any chance that I might be competitive in sports.

There is a plus to the sickness. I became a voracious reader. Despite speaking Pidgin, immersion in books taught me grammar and the meaning of words. Understanding words gave me ideas and concepts that formed the foundation stones for success in life.

Although mental acuity is important, I wanted to avoid being a ninety-eight pound weakling. I tried Charles Atlas's dynamic tension techniques which did not involve running. It was not enough to strengthen my body to overcome the racking cough spells of asthma.

For a year and a half I spent spring, summer, and into the fall bed-ridden. Omnivorous reading led me to the story of Glenn Cunningham, a boy afflicted with a devastating injury to his leg. Despite all odds he overcame his handicap. His story inspired me.

One sunny day I stood on the beach and watched two Filipinos diving in the ocean beyond the protective lagoon. Occasionally, one of them surfaced with a fish on a spear. It excited me. Many times, mother had said, "Your grandfather good fisherman. Maybe you catch fish like him." But our family did not have nets or spears.

When the boys came ashore my heart thumped hard, for they had a string with ten multi-colored fish and a small octopus. "Wow! You some good," I said in Pidgin, meaning that they were great fishermen.

Pete smiled and said, "*Salamat* (thanks)."

"*Kokua* da kine?" I asked. Pidgin for "help me learn spear fishing."

Pete nodded. Over the next several days we assembled the equipment.

"You understand slingshot," Pete said, as he kneeled on the concrete floor of the family garage. "Same idea. Instead of a stick we use hollow bamboo."

Pete fixed strips of rubber onto the bamboo. He tied a cord to each of the loose rubber ends and we had an underwater slingshot.

"Straighten this fence wire. Bend the front end back," Pete said.

I used a vice and pliers to create a prong on one end of the four-foot length of wire. It was not sleek like a sharp pencil. Its pointed end appeared more like a claw hammer, blunt and massive. "No can spear with this," I said.

"*Magaling* (good job)," said Pete. He took a file and rasped metal from the stub end of the spear. Within a half hour he had shaped the blunt head of the wire into a pointed hook.

He released the spear from the vice, eyed its length, and tested the sharpness of its end, nodded, and said, "*Sibat pating.*"

"What?"

"Some good this one. Spear shark with da kine."

The last thing in the world I wanted to meet in the ocean was a shark. Although my grandfather's *aumakua* is that fish, I hadn't learned the art of capturing the spirit of an ancestor and teleporting it into a shark. "Let's just stick with manini," I answered, choosing a small fish twice the size of my hand.

Pete watched me shiver. "What's a mattah you? Go for big game. No scared the shark."

I knew he was trying to frighten me. He succeeded. But a burning desire impelled me to move ahead and try to spear fish. With a slight quaver in my voice I said, "First time, go slow. Fish in the lagoon. Later go over the reef into deeper water."

"Okay, you got goggles?"

I shook my head. I didn't have money to buy them.

Pete withdrew from his pocket glasses set in a wooden frame. "Try."

I did. The underwater goggles sat snug on my face. I was ready to fish.

* * *

It takes a great effort to submerge. Your lungs are like a great bladder and salt water will not let you sink. However, you will drown if you are not smart. By treading water, you can float in the sea for a long time. The trick in spear fishing is to breathe deep, duck below the surface, kick hard, and try to grab onto the coral reef. Not an easy thing to do. The ocean surges push you from your handhold. Seawater forces you up. Your right hand holds a spear. The left hand seeks a nub of coral that you can grasp. Your cloth covered feet kick hard to force you under. Your eyes swivel along the bottom searching for an eel or any dangerous thing that can bite you.

My first day was a disaster. I could not grasp a rock. Buoyancy shoved me to the surface. Waves turned me upside down. I struggled from the surf wheezing, cold, and miserable. It was an ordeal to plod home coughing at every step. My body shaking, mom hustled me into bed. "You have a fever," she said, a worried look on her face. "No more fishing."

Weakness overcame me. Although in a delirium, the momentary glimpses of the life underwater played across my mind. Varied colors, unusual coral shapes, and mysterious things existed under the sea. Animals flitted about in great abundance. I vowed to dive again. "Don't take my spear," I stammered and fell asleep.

Early the next morning, with the sun's light spreading across the horizon, I took my equipment and entered the water. It was low tide. Swimming out to deeper water, my chest scraped the coral reef, seaweed tickled my skin. The water was clean, visibility fading into an azure blue. The suggestion of wonders beyond my sight drew me onward like Dorothy following the yellow brick road in the land of Oz. Though I shivered, it was a glorious time to be at sea. Determination to discover enticed me onward.

Ahead I saw manini, flitting above and around a coral head. Approaching the fish, they dashed into crevices in the rocks, and then rose from their hiding places like green balloons to stare at me. Were they curious or taunting me, doubting my ability to catch them?

I did as Pete taught me, shoved the bamboo tube up the length of the spear until the attached rubber was taut. I pinched the rubber tight to the spear, dove, seizing a rock. Everything was perfect except the spear bent with the tension of the rubber tubing. I failed to twist the strips around the spear to give it extra strength.

Oh, did the manini have a great time whirling and swooping around the coral. Their teasing infuriated me, but I was powerless. My spear was bent into the shape of a V and needed to be straightened. I tried to bend it in the water, but I couldn't remove the kink. I needed a hammer and block of metal to pound out the bend.

With this disaster, I plodded out of the water. Shivering, I hurried home breathing hard from the effort. The asthma wheeze grew louder. Instead of cheers, Mom scolded me and put to bed. Rats!

* * *

Glenn Cunningham at eight years old was burned in a schoolhouse fire. His brother died in the disaster. Doctors recommended his legs be amputated. He had lost all the flesh on his knees and shins and all the toes on his left foot, with its arch destroyed. Glenn said no. The doctors answered that he would never walk again. With grim determination he set out to rehabilitate himself with strenuous exercise and a positive attitude. Cunningham was a medalist in the 1936 Olympics and set world records in the mile and 800 meter run.

Cunningham's story was of a boy who would not give up despite injuries. Glenn almost achieved his goal, a four minute mile. In 1938 he was within .04 of a second of accomplishing the feat. When he failed, experts said humans could never run that fast.

The summer of my ninth year was hell. Rigorous swimming, diving until my ears screamed and my sinuses throbbed. After an ocean adventure, I could not breathe through my nose and had to gulp in air. For an asthma sufferer it was disastrous. Added to these woes were multiple coral cuts to hands, feet, and legs. There was not a day that went by where I did not add a fresh wound to my body.

Pete would tease me, saying, "Scabby kid."

It was true. I looked as if I had lost a fight with multiple razors. My mother worried, but the cuts were superficial, and though iodine stings, it healed the broken skin.

I was not a successful fisherman. It was hard to swim to the floor of the sea, level out, grasp a rock, and with one hand pinching rubber bands against a wire spear, try to shoot a darting fish. But despite the ailments and setbacks, the worse part of spear fishing was quitting the water and have a smart aleck say, "white wash again." I could withstand the "slings and arrows" of coughing and bruises, but to be told you were a failure was the "unkindest cut of all."

Summer dragged to a close. Though I had not achieved the goal of catching fish, I grew stronger. It was no longer to bed after a diving expedition. My breathing, though wheezy, did not lead to crippling coughing.

At the end of August, heavy rains flooded Kapa'a and caused Waitala pond to overflow into the sea. A cousin said, "I think Samoan crabs got washed out." Logic told me that the crustaceans would seek a home in the calm waters of the lagoon.

When the storm subsided and the dirty flood water dissipated, I took my spear and went to the lagoon behind my home. Between the beach and the open sea is a narrow shelf of up-thrust rock paralleling the shore. It acts as a barrier to the heavy pounding of waves and creates a sheltered stretch of water.

Sunlight filtered through the heavy cloud cover. In the distance the horizon streaked blue, a sign that the day would be sunny and glorious. Still, the wind riled the ocean and the outgoing tide clashed with the incoming waves and made the breakers *kiki* (leap up).

Plunging into the cool water, my sight was blurred by the *opala* (trash) from the storm. Not a good time to spearfish. But I needed to be the first in the water, before some *palaualelo* (lazy braggart) stole whatever crab was hiding under the surface. There are those who have *aihue* (larceny) in their hearts and claim whatever was in the lagoon as theirs.

Diving in three feet of water, I slid along the sand heading for crevices in the up-thrust shelf of rock. In the geological past, an earthquake had shoved this narrow quarter-mile finger of stone above the sea, and created the lagoon behind my home.

A slit in the stone loomed in front of me, its innards dark. I placed my hand on an edge to keep my face from being shoved in by an errant wave. My spear hand shook. I peered into the gloom.

There was nothing to catch except sea dust. Surfacing, my heart pounded in my chest. I had never caught a Samoan crab. Those I had seen in the market were red, armored, and displayed huge pincers. What would I do if attacked? Horrid thoughts blazed through my mind. I stood, debating whether to give up the hunt.

I could hear Pete say, "Scaredy cat." Point to my spear and tease, "Whitewash again." Mother would sigh, "Not fisherman like your grandfather."

The water was cold. I could always blame my failure on the chill of the sea affecting my asthma. Deep down inside I would know that it was a lack of courage that caused me to give up.

Another dive, my left hand seized the rock ledge and propelled me to a small cave. Its insides were gloomy. I surfaced for a moment, took a deep breath, and ducked under water. My face filled the opening, my right hand held the spear ready to fire. Murk blotted my sight. Is there something in a far corner of the slit in the shelf?

Sunlight filled the slit. A huge spider-like thing, with eyes popping high above its red shell and massive pincers opening in menace, loomed inside the cave. A sight as scary as Dracula bending down to drink blood.

I reared back, shoveling sand into my nose, scraping my forehead against the shelf. Surfacing, I stepped away from the cave, sneezing out granules of sand.

Willing my shaking body to be calm, I twisted the bamboo tube in my right hand, setting the rubber propellants taut around my spear. I ducked down to the cave. The monster was there sitting in a corner, its lidless eyes glued to mine. Its many feet dug into the sand, whether to scurry or attack, I did not know. I fired my weapon between the pop eyes, stopping the beast in its tracks.

"Victory," I thought and shoved the haft of the spear into the crustacean's body.

Horrors! The animal was crawling the length of the spear toward my face. What to do? Abandon the weapon and flee? But family friend Jack had said, "Never give up your catch whether to the sea or the shark."

I yanked the haft and ran toward the shore. The dense sea water shoved the crab to the pronged end of the spear and I exited the lagoon with my prize twitching its feet and claws in a useless endeavor to escape. Oh, what pride I had when the animal was in the pot and the family praised me for my ability. "Just like your grandfather," Mom said. "Good fisherman."

* * *

Yellow cannery waste stopped flowing into the sea. It signified the end of the grinding season when no more unneeded juice would be dumped into the ocean. It also meant that school would start since young cheap labor was no longer needed to harvest pineapple.

It was the last day to fish before I cracked the books. A summer that had started in hell had become bearable. I could dive for two hours without being sick in bed afterwards. My lungs were stronger and the asthma manageable.

I stood in the ocean, beyond the lagoon, and watched the lake-smooth sea sparkle in the morning sun. It was glorious, a day to conquer whatever I met.

Hunting for an hour fulfilled my expectations. I caught several fish, each one threaded onto a cord attached to a wooden float. I swam toward what I called the "cave hole." It is a brain coral anchored to the reef. The area all around it was relatively flat and the rock I aimed for looked like a huge multi-colored pumpkin sitting in a soccer field.

Manini flitted around the outcropping. Luck was with me, for the fish dove into caves in the stone that tunneled through the coral. Several magnificent dives followed and soon my cord held six fish. Though successful, I worried a little bit because fishermen had told me, "If you stay in one spot, the smell of blood from the speared fish will attract the shark."

"Fiddlesticks," I said, surfacing from a victorious dive. "No worry."

Down I went, kicking hard. I stayed under water peering into the cave. Waiting until the sunlight glinted off fish eyes. I released my spear and skewered the fish, two with one thrust. They rattled the wire against the coral, gyrating in the hole, trying to free themselves. It took time to secure my catch. Air bubbled from my mouth before I could finally pull my bent spear and captured fish from the cave.

Gulping, I glanced at my flopping prizes. A stream of greenish blood flowed from their gills. A slight twinge of fear chilled me. Would this bring mano as I had been warned it would?

"Ah, no worry the shark," friend Jack had said. "If come, jab him in the nose."

Pete had offered the opposite advice, saying, "Shark come, beat water with your feet and hands. Da bugga run away."

Thinking on these pieces of contrary advice I said, "On such a heavenly day how can the devil be near?"

Fifty yards away, knifing towards me through an ocean flat as a pancake, sliced a fin as big as a black sail. In a flash I remembered what a fisherman had told me. "Hammerhead been eating cannery waste dumped in the sea." This had to be that fish, aiming to make a meal out of me.

Heeding Pete's advice I pounded the sea with all four limbs, struggling to reach the lagoon. I was not up to facing a full grown shark with a wire spear.

Though I beat the water with all the strength I could muster, I knew I would not make it before the fatal strike. I released my fish cord, heedless of prior warnings not to feed the shark. "They go into frenzy," Jack had explained.

Exhausted, I stopped splashing water and turned to meet my fate. Oh joy, the fin had disappeared. Pete's advice had saved me. Gulping air, I calmed myself and thrust my head into the water to regain my fish. A large spotted eel slithered from its lair, its rope-shaped body, multi-fanged beak, rearing like a cobra ready to strike my catch.

"Damn," I said. "Enough already." I cocked my spear and fired. The wire hammered into the tube shaped body of the beast, halting its charge, and shoving it out of its hole. You should know this: when an eel bites it will wrap its tail around the coral and fix its teeth-filled jaws on an arm or leg. It will hold tight to what it seizes until killed or you tear away, leaving part of your body in its mouth to be digested for lunch.

Unlike the crab that slithered up my spear, this eel wrapped itself around the wire, biting at the metal. My cord of fish floated nearby and I seized it. Despite my weariness I felt victorious. I had overcome one of the devils of the deep. I had caused mano to flee. Despite these successes, I knew that one day I would face the shark and he would not run.

At home, I reflected on the summer. Reading had helped me. Glenn Cunningham's story was an inspiration to any boy who has a handicap. I realized that like a long distance runner, I had to battle the demons on my own. Only I could make myself better. This was not an egotistical claim, but a realistic one. As my school teacher said, "God helps those who help themselves."

For three months I had struggled, fighting my weakness. But unlike the previous fall, I started school on time and not in bed.

CHAPTER 11

European Grandfathers

Lava bursting from the meeting point of three tectonic plates created the nine islands of the Azores two-thousand-four hundred miles east of New Bedford, Maine, and a thousand miles west of Portugal. In the nineteenth century, the waters surrounding these volcanic islands were swarming with "swimming oil wells." Whales visited on a regular basis. Portuguese men were skilled at harpooning them. New England ship captains sought these men for their ability to capture whales.

A decade after oil was discovered in Pennsylvania, Antonne Fernandez hired onto a whaling ship visiting his home island of Pico. Life on board the vessel was harsh. He had little to eat, his work days long, and the capture of whales dangerous.

Once a whale was sighted, the mother ship launched an eighteen-foot boat. The vessel pursued the animal. Adjacent to it, a long barbed spear pierced its flesh and hooked onto its spine. Then the ordeal began. The whale dove, pulling out thousands of feet of line as it sought to free itself from the harpoon. Sometimes, the injured creature turned on its tormentors, smashed the rowboat, and scattered sailors over the sea.

When the animal was near death, the mother ship hove to and secured it. Then more dangerous work began, the slicing of the animal into strips.

It's like peeling a floating orange. Men stand on a platform above the whale, flensing it while the ship rolls with the waves and wind. Attracted by blood, sharks rip out pieces of the dying beast. Woe to the sailor who falls into the roiling ocean while the feeding frenzy was in progress.

Although whaling in Hawaiian waters was relatively easy, the dangerous experiences are in the Arctic where the large mammals feed and grow fat. Cold winds whip up in an instant and freeze the sea. Two such disasters occurred to the whaling fleets in 1871 and again in 1876. In these catastrophes, dozens of ships were destroyed and scores of men died. The losses could not be recouped. After the last Arctic freeze, Antonne Fernandez jumped ship in Lahaina, Mau'i. He made a home in Makawao, married, and sired my father, William Antonne Fernandez.

My dad grew up nurtured by his grandmother, with Hawaiian his first language. In the meantime, Grandfather took a job as a cowboy at the Parker Ranch on the Island of Hawai'i.

At age eight Antonne took his son and put him to work packing the mail from the ranch to Hilo, a one-hundred-twenty-mile round trip. The task he was assigned was difficult for an unschooled youth. But Grandfather said, "The only good boy is a hard working boy."

There followed seven years of never-ending work. It was too much for Dad. He wanted an education and at fifteen he ran away to Honolulu. The city was in turmoil. A counter revolution against the new Republic had occurred, and royalists were on trial for treason. The deposed Queen, Liliu'okalani, lay in prison and faced the prospect of hanging for her sedition.

In Honolulu, Dad took any job he could and went to school to learn reading, writing, and arithmetic. He eventually became a mounted patrolman and took correspondence courses in business administration. Giving up on police work, he tried various businesses: fish monger, stage coach operator, and haberdasher. But in later life, he would confess that "there was too much on the cuff and too little in the till."

One night he walked the streets of Honolulu and saw an advertisement for "silent movies." He paid his nickel and watched the show. The slapstick pantomime on the screen he could understand even if words weren't spoken. He looked at the audience, a theater filled with the multi-cultured people who had come to work in the sugar fields. They laughed or cried as the players on the screen portrayed their story.

Dad made a deal with the movie owner, learned the trade and acquired equipment needed to operate silent movies on the road. Near the time the Titanic sank, Dad strapped a projector on his back, loaded his wagon and began touring the hundred or more labor camps throughout the Hawaiian Islands showing his movies.

* * *

Joseph Scharsch shook with rage reading the poster announcing the changes Germany made to his homeland, Alsace-Lorraine. Worse, the bulletin proclaimed the beginning of conscription into the German army. Because of the foolish pride of Emperor Napoleon III, France had been induced into a war with Prussia and lost. The price of peace was money and the cession of Alsace to the new nation of Germany.

Joseph did not want to leave his home and family, but he wanted to live in freedom. He, along with other Alsatians, emigrated from their homeland.

Scharsch chose to seek his fortune in America. He worked on a steamer bound for Panama. He crossed the isthmus by rail and headed north for Los Angeles, eventually winding up in San Francisco. An excellent cook, he had no problems finding work as a chef. But wander-lust impelled him west and he came to Honolulu, taking a job at the Royal Hawaiian Hotel.

But the pursuit of cooking did not intrigue Scharsch. Persuaded by a wealthy friend, Joe sailed for Kaua'i and took employment as a field supervisor at Kilauea Plantation. He wanted marriage, a family, and land. A rich land owner, Charles Titcomb, introduced him to thirty pure Hawaiian women. From this bevy, Scharsch chose my grandmother, Julia. With his plantation earnings, he bought acreage from a Hawaiian near the Kilauea River and built a home, meeting hall, and started a farm.

Children came. Prosperity was within his grasp when the plantation crushed Joe's hopes. They announced that the canal dug by the prior owner to sluice water from the river trespassed across plantation land and he must "cease and desist." Litigation ensued and Scharsch eventually lost his case. His property landlocked, he gave it up and moved to Kapa'a.

I mention this since it shows the power of the plantations before World War II. They controlled the government and refused to accept the traditional Hawaiian right to access water when needed. It took a ton of water to produce a pound of sugar. This meant that the business interests sought control of as much of the water courses as they could.

Grandfather Scharsch took a job at Kealia Sugar, a mill near home. He believed in education, but primarily for his two eldest sons. He put his daughter, Agnes, to work at the new cannery that opened in 1913 in Kapa'a. Her earnings financed the schooling of her two brothers in Honolulu. Her education stopped at the third grade.

Despite my mother being put to work at an early age, my French grandfather preached education for men as a means of achieving success in life. This credo rang true for many immigrants who entered into labor contracts to work in the sugar fields. Though all hands were needed to work and produce money, the laborers who had families urged their children to go to school and advance themselves through education.

* * *

Growing up on Kaua'i, the inability of the Hawaiian to cope with the sugar plantation world of profit making was evident. Their troubles were compounded by alcohol. Across the street from my home lived a Hawaiian family composed of a dozen children and elders living in a small house. Despite existing a step above destitution they were generous with what they had. "*E komo mai i ka paina* (Come and eat)," was a common call when I visited them.

The living room of the sparsely furnished home was not big enough for all who were invited. The eating place chosen was the dirt floor of the family garage. A woven mat of lauhala covered the ground with calabashes of food spread upon it. Neighborhood kids and family members ranged themselves along the mat, dipping into the poi bowls. Like the others, I plunged my fingers into the goop, twirling them until they slimed with grey paste, then down my throat went the poi. Three or four finger poi was the best. Aged until sour, it puckers the mouth when swallowed.

Some Hawaiian families lived without societal restraints. This was true with those who lived across the street from my home. The father of the family or maybe the mother's boyfriend, I was never sure of the big man's connection to my neighbors, would come home late at night drunk on whiskey. Then terror struck as he went into a rage and beat up the women in the house. Children scattered from the building like frightened rabbits. Several came to our porch to hide behind its railing. I spent more than one night hugging my shaking friend Ambrose waiting for the police to come and quell the neighborhood bashing.

Off to the local lockup would go the drunken man where he might spend a week or a month confined to jail. But when he was released it would only be a matter of time before the next violent explosion occurred. I did mention that the home was sparsely furnished. In his drunken rages the Hawaiian had broken all the furniture the family had.

By contrast, my dad did not drink alcohol or coffee, nor did he smoke. He refused to take drugs of any kind, including medicine. He was a health addict and forbade unhealthy indulgences. As an example, both parents did not like the Hawaiian way of eating from the same calabash. My father would say, "Don't use your fingers. Put your food on your plate and eat with your knife and fork." After dining, the dishes had to be washed in hot water and put away. Cleanliness and sanitation was preached at home. We did not have an outhouse.

I am not saying these things to be disparaging of Hawaiians or to extol the way my family lived. We were poor in comparison with the wealthy plantation folks, who lived in pretentious estates from which we were excluded. Unfortunately, many Hawaiians did not hold steady jobs, but instead subsisted on catching products from the sea, raising animals, and making what they needed. It was not unusual to find families on the north shore of Kaua'i living in the same way as their ancestors.

Who can blame them for wanting to live without constraints? The island exerts a hypnotic charm on anyone living on Kaua'i. Rain cleans the air. The sky is blue. The land is drenched with sunlight. The ocean waves sweep the shore in a steady unchanging rhythm. A daily opiate that dulls the senses and causes a languorous indolence where one can forget being stressed by responsibilities.

Unfortunately, I was pulled from my childhood apathy by the European side of my family. "Wear shoes. Cover up your nakedness. You're too dark."

"I don't care," I said.

"Don't talk back" was the answer, followed by smacks on the bottom.

Despite my protests I was forced to learn. But I would much rather have been a fisherman and challenged the might of the sea, and led a simple stress-free life.

CHAPTER 12

An Invisible Force

Herbert Hoover promised Americans "a chicken in every pot and a car in every garage." But soon after his election the stock market crashed and a "Great Depression" struck our country. It was during the leanest year of this economic downfall that I was born.

Growing up, I did not understand the destitution that affected the American continent, because ordinary folks in Hawai'i lived in a continuing state of economic depression. We traded, built what was needed by hand, or did without.

Dictating our lives was an invisible force. As I grew older, I learned that this great power was called "The Big Five." These companies, founded during the missionary period of the nineteenth century, controlled the economy and government of the islands since the time of the overthrow of the Hawaiian kingdom in 1893. It was their credo that civil disorder shall not interfere with the making of profits. They were opposed to unionization since it meant higher labor costs.

When I first saw NRA I didn't realize that the words stood for "National Recovery Act." But I knew when I saw it and heard the men whispering, that the words and eagle symbol meant unionization and fair pay for workers.

I also heard men speak of the forceful suppression of strikers. At some time in the past, violence and deaths had occurred because of unionization. Workers in the plantation towns did not dare speak the "union" word, for the sugar people had spies among the laborers who reported any dissension. But in my town, everyone knew each other and there were no spies. In Kapa'a, men spoke of collective bargaining and labor relations.

Unfortunately, there were sinful aspects to being a free town. After Franklin Delano Roosevelt was elected, prohibition ended, liquor became available, and a taxi-dance hall opened. I suppose there is nothing wrong in charging for a dance, but for a laborer starved for the companionship of a woman, it was a sure way to give up a week's wages strutting on the dance floor.

Despite being warned by my elders to stay away, I wanted to watch the action. Pete knew a secret path to the dance hall and he led me through bushes to our destination. Though blinded by the dense foliage, loud music guided us. Arriving at the ballroom, we peeked in. The sun barely lit the room. A Puerto Rican three-piece band played tinkling music, a tune I did not recognize. A half-dozen couples danced across the floor. The women clothed in skimpy dresses. The men, mostly Filipinos, wore outfits of pink, purple, or wine pants and rainbow-colored shirts. Each dancing man wanted to have the look of his favorite rooster.

Seated in chairs along the walls were men waiting their turn. Some bounced to and fro, keeping time with the catchy music. Others whistled and made cat calls as dancers displayed spectacular moves. The noise became thunderous when a woman's skirt flew up, revealing her white legs and thighs.

"These guys are really hard up," Pete said. "They'll go for anything that wears lipstick. Some will pay thirty to fifty dollars in a night."

"How much a dance?"

"A dime."

"You mean some guy will spend money for three hundred or five hundred dances?"

Pete gave me a strange look, then said, "Girls get paid the big money for putting out. You watch. When you see the hand stroking the butt a deal's been made. If she takes the hand and moves it up her back, then no deal."

What did Pete mean? Is there something else besides dancing that went on in the hall?

The music stopped and the women rapidly disengaged, moving to reserved seats near the orchestra. Within a few moments men came to them, offering tickets. A girl would select a partner and then proceed to the dance floor. One lady declined all offers and sat out two dances until a young Filipino-Hawaiian entered the hall.

"I know that guy." I said.

"Yeah, so do I. That gal over there must be the one he has been banging." Pete pointed to the woman who declined dances. She stood up and hurried toward our mutual friend, her face wreathed in a smile.

"Some guys have all the luck," Pete said, his face twisted into a grimace. "The story is she is carrying his baby."

"What? He's not even sixteen."

"And she is older than him."

"Having a baby without marriage is a sin!"

"People sin all the time when they're in love."

I guess that's the answer. When in love you forget the consequences.

* * *

My dad operated the Rialto Theater with a stipulation from the powers that be that only "wholesome entertainment" be shown. Creosote covered the floors and walls to retard termites, making the theater dark and staining my feet brown as I ran barefoot through the movie house. Smoking was prohibited for fear of fire. Highly combustible movie film can turn show houses into burning infernos.

Outside of the movies and taxi dancing there was no other entertainment, not even music from a radio or gramophone. For those who loved glitz, Kapa'a was a dull town with drunkenness as the primary crime.

In the late nineteenth century, Chinese planters found the marsh land to the west of the "Solid" ideal for rice growing. Their efforts resulted in the growth of a small community of Chinese who built homes and established businesses. By my time, the Chinese rice fields were gone with the evidence of the past prosperity being a rice warehouse, a bunk house for working men, and Chinese merchant houses lining the government highway.

Four generations of Chinese had grown up in Kapa'a, all living in compounds or in second-story tenements above the family store. Their development of the town was evident from the businesses established on the main road. The first immigrants had been laborers or adventure seekers arriving without wives. It was not uncommon for these men to marry Hawaiian, the only women available to them. But, once prosperous, these rice farmers imported picture brides from China who brought with them ancient customs like foot binding for infant girls. It was a terrible practice which produced severe pain for the child through the breaking of the natural arch of the feet.

This first generation of Chinese men who came to Kapa'a eliminated their queues, long braided strands of hair mandated by the Emperor of China. They rid themselves of what I call the Fu Manchu look, colored pajama clothes, and stringy Satanic beards. They adopted American clothing of shoes, khaki pants, and a short-sleeve white or blue shirt.

A total of nine canneries were built during the pineapple era in Hawai'i. Two were located in or near Kapa'a. Pono Cannery, begun in 1913, kick-started my town from shanties to a community of well built structures and homes.

Immigrant Japanese brought to work sugar fields in the late nineteenth century left the plantations and sought employment with the cannery or started service businesses in the town and surrounding area. They would become the primary laborers in the pineapple growing fields located north of Kapa'a.

One group of Japanese from Okinawa became independent farmers growing pineapple in the hinterland near the town. Needing an outlet for their crop, they convinced a venture capitalist to start Hawaiian Fruit Packers in Kapahi in the foothills of Kapa'a. The cannery superintendent was Walter Smith, related to me through the marriage of his brother to my aunt. The "invisible force" tried to suppress this independent enterprise but failed to do so.

Although Japanese immigration had been halted by American fear of the "Yellow Peril," forty percent of the Kaua'i population was Japanese. First-generation immigrants tended to be clannish and insisted on their children respecting ancestors and marrying Japanese. Second- generation children were friendly and easy to get along with. They were good in sports and adept at martial arts called jujitsu. But when young men broke the unwritten rule, and married outside of their race, there was trouble with the new wife who was expected to follow the rules laid down by mama san.

Many Japanese families settled in Kapa'a and their presence was reflected in the establishments that they opened, fish markets, grocery stores, and mercantile shops. Language could be a barrier to shopping, but Pidgin always worked.

After the Philippines became American territory, the plantations hired Ilocano and Visayan workmen who replaced Chinese and Japanese in the fields. When their sugar employment ended, these men came to Kapa'a, opening a pool hall, barber shop, and stores. The plantations had barred Filipino workers from bringing women and children. Kapa'a, being a free town, meant that Filipino businessmen could find letter wives from their homeland or marry Hawaiian.

Portuguese imported from Madeira and the Azores brought their wives and children. They were well-schooled people who learned English rapidly and became the plantation work specialists and supervisors. When finished with their sugar jobs, they came to Kapa'a and served as teachers, mechanics, and administrators.

Although there were Old World animosities between the disparate people, in Kapa'a hostilities between races did not exist. All had to work together, for everyone had little and cooperation between ethnic groups was necessary for survival.

It was different in a plantation town. The working races were kept separated. The necessities were purchased from the company store. Plantation regulations dictated life in the labor camps.

Though we were a free town of mixed races, the powerful presence of the invisible force was felt when we saw the "no trespass" signs, the "*Sabidong*" warnings, and the barring of passage to the sea for Hawaiians to exercise traditional gathering rights. Add to this two railroad tracks passing through the town without any warning signs, devices to control traffic, or protection of children from the dangers. Without governmental restraints, plantations destroyed the environment by dredging up coral which altered the shoreline, blew up reefs, and introduced pests to combat rats in the sugar fields.

It was useless to protest these actions. The Big Five controlled everything.

CHAPTER 13

The North Shore

Primitive, barbaric, back country, these words describe northern Kaua'i. I watched a lush tropical jungle pass by as we motored around a winding roadway heading for Ha'ena.

"Don't drive so fast," my mother complained as our car came perilously close to the edge of the unfenced roadway. Through shrubs and trees anchored to a sheer earth wall, I caught glimpses of a yellow sand beach five hundred feet below.

"Beautiful ocean," I said.

"Dangerous! Big currents take you out to sea," my mother answered, dampening my enthusiasm to jump from the car, crash through the foliage, and land in the water. Our vehicle sped down the hill heading for a small bay sparkling in the sun.

"Look, just like King Kong Island," I said, hopping up and down in my car seat as perpendicular mountains overgrown with jungle loomed ahead. I visualized the monster crashing through the trees, seizing our car, and hurling it into the bay where a sluggish stream poured brown water into the sea. The gigantic ape movie had just played at the Rialto and the images from it were vivid in my mind.

On we plunged into the bowels of a lush dark forest. Water dripped from the trees after an early morning rain. A light mist hovered between the trees. "Oh," I said, "looks like the big lizard coming. Where are the gas bombs?" In my mind I saw the giant brontosaurus plunging through the trees, its long neck and ugly face filled with sharp teeth. You have to see the movie to understand the impressions I had on my first trip to Ha'ena. We are in Kong's land where the gigantic beasts rule supreme.

After visiting a spooky cave, where Mother said, "Don't take the stones, ancestors buried here," we headed for the end of the road and the trail along the Na Pali coast. At Ke'e Lagoon, I stared at miles of two-thousand-foot stone walls that plunged into the sea.

"Hawaiians used to climb Makana," said my mother, pointing to a peak shaped like the brow and face of King Kong. "They would throw down burning sticks into the sea. The fire fall is beautiful at night."

"Yeah, and they would cast naked maidens to the sharks," quipped cousin Pono.

"Wash your mouth with chili pepper," said Aunt Katie. "Bad say things like that in front of small boy."

Her words were too late. I visualized Fay Wray plunging naked toward the sea. Would Kong save her? In my imagination, a hairy hand reached out and grasped the blonde woman before she fell into the ocean. The cliff coast of Kaua'i will do that to you. It is primitive, mysterious, and Jurassic.

"Just above Ke'e lagoon was a hula heiau," my mother said. "In the old days, it was considered the finest school in all the islands."

"People came from all of Hawai'i to learn," said Aunt Katie. "Hard work. The training required physical strength and discipline. You gave up family and happiness so you could learn without interruption."

"Pele's sister Laka is the goddess of the hula. She loves mysterious places. That's why the *kumu* (teachers) chose this windswept spot beneath Makana," my mother said.

"Can I go on the trail over the mountains?" I begged, hoping to see the cliffs of Na Pali.

"Put your sneakers on," Mom said. "Pono, you go with him and no further than Hanakapi'ai."

All I needed was permission and I rushed to the car, laced on the shoes and ran to the base of the mountain. "Wait!" the women chorused.

Pono came to me and said, "Stay close. Watch the edge. Trail is narrow." Off he climbed, hiking up flat rock boulders set in steps up the side of Makana.

Using legs and hands, I pushed, crawled, jumped up the rock strewn trail leading to the valleys of the Na Pali coast. Hundreds of feet above the beach we paused to catch our breath. Waves curled toward the rock walls smashing into the reef sheltering the lagoon and dashing into the solid stone face of the mountain. The ocean's magnificent power was on display as brisk wind swept from the water and howled around my ears.

"Powerful current down there," Pono said. "You get caught in it and next stop is Japan."

We pushed on up the trail. The blackness of Makana rose above us, its steep side patched with green moss, tufts of ferns, and flowers thrusting from the rock wall. On our right, the trail's edge plunged toward a deep blue sea. Small hala trees and shrubs clung to the descending cliff face. They would only slow a fall into the ocean and not stop it.

After what Pono judged to be a thousand feet of climbing, the trail bent to the left and as we made the turn the wind whipped into me. I grabbed my cousin's leg, otherwise I would be blown like a scrap of paper over the edge and into the sea. The sight that greeted my eyes was a feast of beauty.

Sunlight played on the roiling sea flecked with foaming waves racing like lines of dancers bouncing in rhythmic cadence toward the cliff walls stretching out as far as I could see. The continuous rolling movement of the water was hypnotic and I closed my eyes to break the spell. When I dared to look again I saw far below a brown turtle drifting lazily on the sea. I thought that I could reach out and grasp it, the creature was so big. But it's an illusion. The animal was far beyond my reach.

Above the turtle soared a white bird. Its cawing echoing off the cliff walls added to the frightening sounds of howling winds and rustling leaves. Rising from the sea, it glided high to the pointed tops of the cliffs a thousand feet above my head. Along the great walls of clinging moss and ferns the bird flew, then plummeted two thousand feet. Skimming over the waves, it fled out of sight.

We began our descent amidst cascading waterfalls that sprayed fresh water along the trail and flowed over the edge into the ocean. I was awed by the beauty of Na Pali. I understood why the hula masters chose this place to teach, for the cliff coast breathes spirituality. It was a place where you live with the gods of ancient times.

Pono was ahead of me and reached the floor of a valley. A stream ran along its narrow length. Taro stalks grew in the water. Abundant hala trees, their leaves coned like umbrellas, kept the valley in shadow. I heard the thunder of waves and fear gripped me, for the sound of their crashing echoed through the valley.

"This is Hanakapi'ai. It is named for the menehune queen who died here when her people sought to escape the tyranny of the Tahitians."

"You mean there really were little people who lived on Kaua'i?

Pono's faced wreathed in a smile. "You've seen the fishpond they built in Lihue and the stone-lined ditch in Waimea. There once were little people on the island. But they all left because of oppression and escaped to a new land by way of this valley."

I looked at the pounding waves smashing onto the sand beach, the steepness of the hills surrounding Hanakapi'ai. I could not believe that menehunes could have launched canoes from this site. But like all legends, you accept what you are told since accomplishing the impossible is what makes a story interesting.

* * *

After our hike, the family headed back, passing through Hanalei Valley where thousands of sprouts thrust above the water in dozens of muddy ponds. "Poi from these fields the best," Aunt Katie said.

"No more Chinese," Pono said. "Before, many *Pake* planted rice. Valley covered with paddies. All gone now."

"And before them taro grew in the valley," my mother said.

What happened? Someone mentioned that coffee grew on the hills above Hanalei, but the plants no longer existed. Why?

As I pondered these thoughts, we drove past the low hills of Princeville, a wild stretch of wavy ground once planted in sugar cane. But the mill and its fields vanished. Why?

We dipped down into Wainini beach, its wide and long fringing reef foaming along its edge as waves broke against the fan-shaped shelf of rocks. From the breakers to the shore the water is still. Wainini means "quiet water." A man poled a dugout canoe on a mirror smooth sea. Huge stands of hau trees fringed the shore, yellow blossoms falling into the water making golden sailboats floating lazily along the shoreline.

Shacks and shanties sprouted like tall dried brown shrubs along a flat stretch of green ground bordering the hard-packed sand road. Scattered among the rundown buildings I saw the oxidized red color of rusting cars matching the ochre hills beyond them. Pigs' high-pitched "oinks" disturbed my ears.

"Just like *Hurricane* movie," I said.

"You mean it looks like Tahiti." Pono laughed.

"Yeah, all run down. Everything broken. Stuff all over," I answered, as island scenes from the movie starring Jon Hall and Dorothy Lamour raced through my head.

"Hawaiians got nothing," said Aunt Katie. "We are lucky." She stopped talking as the car pulled into one of the falling-down homes. Numerous children came out from somewhere, giggling. They were barely clothed, several with torn shirts or shorts.

"Come inside," called an old lady dressed in a drab sack and standing at a kitchen door. "Come, eat."

"Only stay short time," said Mother. "We came for dry *akule* and *he'e*."

The women spoke together in Hawaiian, a language that I had not been taught since the Big Five suppressed it. I wandered towards the pig pen, enticed there by the children who kept saying, "Come see."

Behind a shed was a wire enclosure with huge porkers wallowing in mud. Scraps of papaya, bananas, and cooked rice filled the eating troughs of the animals. A malodorous smell mixed with their grunting and I saw, near the pig sty, a long bench with two heart-shaped holes carved out. "Stinky," I said.

"You want see?" said a boy.

I shook my head. Marching back to the car, I wondered how delicious cooked pork could come from such a filthy smelly place. One of my favorite meals was pig's feet, a sweet syrupy concoction of pork fat. After watching cloven hoofs buried in slime, I began rethinking my choice of favorites.

The women had concluded their talk and we were ready to go. With dried fish and octopus wrapped in ti leaves, we headed out. Our auto chugged up a low hill leaving Wainini, then immediately descended into the *ahapua'a* of Kalihiwai. A classic living area of ancient Hawaiians, a pie-shaped valley nature cut from the rock, with a meandering stream emptying into the ocean. In bygone times, fields of taro and sweet potatoes filled the land between the ridges. Extensive copses of sugar cane grew amongst them. The leaves of the cane might be used to thatch the shack roofs or used to form a wind break. Hawaiians did not know how to make molasses from the cut stalks.

A gorgeous crescent of sand cupped an ocean rolling in lazy waves into the bay of Kalihiwai. A thick wood of pine trees lined the road. Huts, shacks, and plantation-style homes lay along the seashore. Draped fishing nets dried on long racks in the sun. At the grass-line along the shore stood rowboats and outrigger canoes, their snouts pointing like bird dogs toward the sea, ready for action when a school of fish came into the bay.

Our car pulled into the yard of a white-painted red-roofed home set in a green lawn bordered by flower beds. The neat home stood in stark contrast to the little Tahiti we had just left. Our Chinese-Hawaiian cousins enjoyed a modicum of prosperity.

A lovely middle-aged woman stepped out of the home, a smile wreathing her face. Clothed in a thin print dress that flowed loosely from her shoulders to her feet, very little flesh showed, for the missionaries taught Hawaiian women to "hide your nakedness."

"*Como mai*, come inside," she said.

"Where's John?" Mother asked.

The lady laughed. "Where else would he be than up on that orange hill?" She pointed. "He has been studying the water for days. The akule not swimming into the bay."

"Too far out?" asked Aunt Katie.

"Yes. He begs and pleads for them to come in. Even says prayers. But no luck."

"Maybe he should pray to the old gods?" said Pono, smiling broadly.

Casting a surreptitious eye to mounds of scattered stones beyond the pine hedge, the woman said in a whisper, "We are Christians."

I knew that the gods of the ancients had been overthrown before the missionaries came, and the open-air temples of rectangular rock walls abandoned and even in some cases destroyed. But I sensed from the looks of the women that there still existed a belief in the efficacy of the *kahuna*.

"Can I go up the hill and see Uncle John?" I asked, breaking into a silence that had lasted for several moments.

"Yes. Run up the road. Trail goes up the orange hill."

"Pono, go with him," Mother said.

The two of us trotted up the road, heading for John's lookout. We found the narrow trail that wound up an ochre red hill and discovered John staring out to sea. Trudging toward him, I heard uncle beg, "Come in. Please come in." I thought he was addressing me, but his hands were motioning to the ocean in a clear sign that he wanted whatever existed out there to swim into the bay.

We came to the older man. Partially bald, with a ruddy face, browned by the hot sun to burnished tan, he gave us a suspicious stare with eyes penetrating through brows of thick white hair. Of medium height, he tended toward the portly. Sparsely dressed in khaki shorts and white short-sleeved shirt, you could tell his Chinese blood by the cut of his eyes.

"Any fish?" Pono asked.

John whispered in a hoarse voice, "Out there," he pointed, adding, "too far."

"Can you show me?" I begged.

"Look. See the dark red spot as the water turns from blue to dark blue?"

Try as I might, I could not penetrate the azure water and find the big-eyed scad, the *akule*.

"Where?"

"See. There."

"Can't see."

"I'll lift you," Pono said.

John gave a look of disgust. I felt that he sought an excuse to quit his perch and go home. "Bad luck you come up hill. Scare the fish away," he grumbled.

"We didn't do anything," I said, trying to balance on Pono's shoulders.

"Come down before you fall down and your mother blames me," John answered.

"We go," and he started down the path towards home, his feet kicking up sprays of red dust.

When we reached home my aunt and mother stood from their seats in the parlor, ready to leave. They had delivered their gifts of poi and pork. "It's late. We need to go," Mother said. "Any chance of a *hukilau?*"

"Maybe," John answered. "Fish inching in. Two, three days. We'll send word."

His answer sparked eagerness inside me that I couldn't suppress. "Can I come see?"

For the first time that day, John smiled. "You come. Be a great fisherman like your grandfather."

We headed home from Kalihiwai, my heart pounding. Uncle promised that I would be like my grandfather. I must be a part of the *hukilau.*

CHAPTER 14

Hukilau

Huki means pull and *lau* means net. Literally, the word means "to pull in the net." It would appear to be an easy task, but it is not. It takes all the ingenuity of fishermen and the cooperation of the local community to pit their combined power against the might of the sea, the animals in it, and the traps that exist beneath the surface.

Word came from Kalihiwai, a huge school of akule had moved into the bay and I should come. With Jack I headed north. *Makani* the wind blew gently. Roosters did not crow their call of, "the sun is coming."

Chafing at the slowness of our progress, I shuffled my bare feet on the floorboard of the Model T Ford, trying to push it faster. Heat from the laboring engine forced my legs up and onto the car seat. Our chugging auto rocked like a baby's crib. Coupled with the early hour and the auto's warmth, I fell asleep.

Cold air blew over my face. Light peeped above the horizon. The engine no longer rumbled. I shook myself awake. Saw the path leading up to John's lookout. Banging shut the door, I ran to the trail and climbed the red-orange hill.

Akana stood with Jack. "Not sure. Maybe false alarm."

Damnation, I thought, we had come all this way for nothing.

Spying me, he said: "Where you get this *lau hau*? He brought bad luck. His shorts are red."

I am about to retort that I am not a vagabond, my shorts are not red, and I did not bring bad luck. I held my tongue. This ritual of insults puts me in my place at the lowest rung of the pecking order of fishermen. Only by proving myself as worthy could I advance and escape the status of being *lau hau*.

John shifted his attention to the sea. Staring into the water, he sought the great maroon blot of akule. Darkness shrouded the water. Even my untrained eye could tell we needed sunlight.

Wandering on the hill, I spied *lanalana*, the spider, weaving her web. Droplets of dew clung to the sticky mesh. Sunlight bursting from a cloudless horizon sent shafts of light across the ocean, striking the dew. Scores of tiny rainbows appeared.

"Look, Uncle John." I pointed at the web. "A good omen."

But the old man dismissed my prediction with a toss of his head and turned back to the sea. The growing light brightened the ocean as the burning orb of *La* thrust above the horizon.

"Pack is spiking. Coming in," Jack said.

"Go," John answered.

"Let me stay and watch from the hill."

Jack did not argue with my choice, but headed for his car. He cranked the engine, with a pop, it back-fired like a rice farmer's shotgun. He cranked again. The engine chugged to life and he drove down the hill to the shacks lining the beach.

"Where's the akule?"

John pointed at the ocean. "No look on the surface. Try look deep."

I strained my eyes, seeking the fish. The sun kept brightening the sea. But I saw nothing. I despaired of ever finding them. If I cannot spot fish then I remain *lau hau*. My eyes smarted with the strain of keeping them wide. I dared not blink for fear of losing the spot John had pointed to.

A spurt of red lightning flashed in the sea. It drew back, and I saw the pile of fish. "What is happening?"

"Big fish hitting small fish. See the large circle spike, then come together?"

"Yes!" burst from my mouth. "I see the ball of akule spurting out, coming together, spike again. What's happening?"

"Big fish, sharks, hitting the pile. They're driving fish to shallow water."

I could see that the maroon spot had taken the shape of a whirling star. The hunted fish swam into the bay to escape the hunters.

On the beach, two rowboats piled high with nets stood poised. Men rested by them waiting for John's signal. None wanted to spring the trap until the animals swam close enough into the bay to be caught. Fish sense the presence of man and will flee when threatened. I have experienced their fright during many hours of underwater spear fishing, easier to catch them hiding in a cave than in open water.

"They're coming in, time to go?" I ask.

"What do you know?" John said, continuing to stare at the water.

I am still *lau hau*. He has put me in my place, at the bottom rung of the ladder. I do not have the experience to judge the time to strike. But the tide rises. The waves grow bigger. The wind freshens. Difficulties mount the longer we wait. A *hukilau* has been given up because conditions changed from optimal to disastrous.

With startling suddenness, John grasped ti leaves shaped like green paddles, waved them, and bellowed, *"Hele mai! Hele mai!"*

The signal to go, go. Below, fishermen grasped the gunwales of boats, slid them on the sand up and over waves crashing onto shore. Pointed snouts of two boats thrust into the water. Men leaped in. Oars flashed out, dipped into the sea, and pushed the vessels into cresting waves threatening to shove the crafts onto the sand. Heaving their wooden blades against the oar locks, the fishermen propelled their boats out to sea, seeking smoother water. One boat paid out net while two men on shore hung onto ropes attached to it.

"Hele mai!" John yelled, his voice pleading. Anxiety spread across his face. His body shook.

Why?

I stared at the sea and understood his worry. The dark ball stopped spiking. Fish no longer moved toward the shore. Did the predators sense the coming of man and called off their attacks?

The boat, paying out net, struggled to keep its prow moving out to sea. Buffeting waves pushed it to the left.

"No!" John cried. "Straight, straight!" He waved his long-stemmed ti leaves forward.

"They can't hear you," I said for I saw the men struggling to control their boats. But I am ignored as children often are.

Ti leaves whipped into the wind. John hopped from foot to foot. "Faster, we will lose the fish."

In the bay, the maroon ball floated with the surge of the sea. Despite the efforts of the fishermen, their boats had not gone beyond the spot staining the water like dark ink spilled onto a blue blotter.

On the beach, men and women gathered. Children shrieked, rushing for the waves. Parents ran after them, drawing them from the sea. Playing in the water could frighten the fish. For these poor people, gifts from the ocean meant survival.

Incrementally, the spot moved closer to shore. The boat paying net moved past the horde of fish.

"Too deep," John muttered.

I wanted to ask a question but decided not to. John had more to worry about than what I might jabber.

Exploding like a lighted sparkler on Christmas Eve, the blot spiked in all directions then came together, closer to shore. John waved his ti leaves to the left, shouting, *"Huli, huli."*

Responding, the net boat turned, beginning the surround of the fish.

"Auwe," John said. The float line had disappeared under water.

The conical-shaped pieces of wood strung along the top rope like beads on a necklace had been pulled beneath the surface by the weights attached to its bottom meshes. Fish could escape over the net barrier.

The spiking stopped. Had the predators gorged themselves full? Did the akule recognize their danger?

The lead boat stopped, its net nearly gone. The second boat came to it. Fishermen began sewing nets together. John ranted, "Hurry up, hurry up. You too slow, fish going to get away."

But we both knew that it's not an easy task to couple nets in a roiling sea. What had been laid heaved with each swell. Boats smashed together from the surge. Men grappled the vessels with their hands to keep them steady. Despite nature's efforts to save her fish, the sewing continued until the second boat disengaged and began paying out net.

Face red, his voice animated with emotion, John yelled, *"Hele mai,"* waving his ti leaves like a sailor giving semaphore signals. Heeding his cry, oarsmen pulled against the sea. Net flowed, disappearing below the surface.

I followed John's eyes. They fixed on a spot within the partial curve of the net. An enormous mass of fish spread out like a red pancake in the shallow water of Kalihiwai Bay. Instead of moving out to sea, the akule drifted closer to shore. A crescent of net, shaped like a giant horseshoe, slowly formed around the fish.

"Hurry, please hurry," John begged, his hands shaking ti leaves like a gale had whipped into them. With a sudden vehemence, he yelled: *"Huli,"* and turned his body toward the broad beach below.

Depositing net, the boat turned. Slowly, the last arm of the crescent built toward shore. Ocean swells surfed the vessel toward the sand. Fishermen flung mesh into the sea. John stopped waving leaves and raced down the hill.

I choked a cry of "Wait for me." I realized that Uncle had more important things to do than tend to a *lau hau* kid.

Running toward level ground, I saw someone leap from the boat holding onto ropes. On the shore a community of helpers rushed into the water and dragged the net onto the beach, completing the surround.

Laboring for breath, John came to the fishermen. Red in the face, I thought he might collapse. But, although winded, he composed himself and said, "How deep?"

"Not sure, maybe five fathoms."

"Net not high enough. What do you think? Maybe put a second net inside the first?"

"Don't know, could spook the fish. Try pulling the net in slow until the float line rises to the surface."

John nodded in agreement.

Attracted to the bay by the news of the *hukilau*, scores of multi-racial people thronged the beach. They had come as immigrants to work the sugar fields. Once their contracts were up they had become farmers and fish folk seeking freedom from the regulations of the plantation.

On both ends of the net, orders were given. Some people to bend low and pull in the lead line, others to keep the net taut by hauling in the float line above it.

"Don't pull hard," John bellowed. "Net can snag on reef."

A surging sea created chaos, sweeping people into the water. Although I sank my feet into the sand, I could barely hold the net. Trapped fish smashed against the mesh, forcing other workers and me into the ocean.

"Keep the lead line down," John yelled, urging those still standing to push their feet into the net and force the mesh under the sand.

Joining with others, I forced the lead line down. A wave smashed onto the shore, knocking me over. The net surged and people fell into the water. We rose laughing like children frolicking on the sea shore. Collectively we came to the net, pushed down on the lead line, shoving it into the sand.

"*A'ole huki*. Stop pulling!" a shout boomed above the sound of the waves. I knew the lead line had snagged on the coral bottom.

"You, you," John pointed. "Get in the canoe, find the holdup."

Jack and another young man paddled along the outer edge of the net, pulling on the float line, searching for the tangle. I watched them free dive. Not an easy task, for they had no duck fins, weight belts, or scuba gear. More than one diver drowned at the ocean bottom, strangled in the net.

I worried for Jack. My family came to me. Aunt Kate said, "Nobody *huki*. Why?"

"Net snagged on rocks. Boys are diving to free it."

My aunt frowned, saying, "*Auwe*. Plenty *pilikia*."

"Lots of trouble if can't free the net. The big school of fish could get away,"

Adults on shore waited for the signal to "*huki*." Despite the need to acquire fish, I saw no anxiety. Tomorrow could prove to be a better day.

"Pull the lead line," someone shouted.

Bending, a score of people dragged in the lower rope.

"Pull the float line," John yelled.

After a short pause he said, "*Huki, huki*."

Others took up his cry. "*Huki*," adults and children shouted. Like barge pullers hauling in rope we chanted, "*Huki, huki, huki*."

The circle of mesh became smaller. The spot that had been maroon in the deep water glinted with silver. The school of trapped fish was huge. As the pack grew denser and shark fins flashed amidst them, John yelled, "*Pau huki!*"

At his command, pulling stopped. Some children wandered into the water but anxious mothers pulled them back. Danger still lay beneath the surface.

John issued directions. Soon a second boat loaded with net pushed into the sea, surrounding the horde again.

I asked Jack, "What's up?"

"Uncle thinks there is too much fish. If we pull all in, markets flooded with akule. Worse, the pile of fish could break the net. He will lay a third net. We pull in some fish trapped in the first net. We leave the rest caught in the second and third nets to live a few more days while the fish sellers come and we arrange to ship akule to Honolulu." Then Jack winked. "Uncle is one smart *Pake*. If he dumps all this fish on the market today, the price goes way down. If he gives out a little at a time, then make money."

Oh, that was disappointing. "I guess I'll miss the party after the *hukilau* is over," I said.

"No worry," Jack answered. He went to help pull in the first net. I did, too. Cooperating with other people was fun for everyone. When the net drew closer to shore and the blob in the water became squirming living things, I became excited. Fish would be given for pulling in the net. My tummy rumbled. I could taste the akule, salted and deep fried.

Drawn in by the pulling, the net shrank like a balloon releasing air. The water turned dark green with thousands of fish trapped within it. Fishermen came with wicker baskets, dipped them in, and hauled out flapping fish that flicked scales everywhere. A fin surfaced from the dense pack. Someone reached in and pulled out a small shark, tossing it onto the sand. It flopped and spanked the yellow beach until a Chinese came and took it away to make shark fin soup.

Shadows lengthened across the ground. Uncle John called a halt to fish sales and divided fish. Anyone who put a hand on the *lau*, man, woman, or child, received a share of the catch. People rushed to gather baskets, sacks, or cords and returned to the beach as John placed even piles of fish onto the sand. As darkness descended, the people left with enough food to feed families for days to come. Most of the akule would be salted and dried, some eaten that night.

I hung back from the gathering wondering if I, a *lau hau*, was worthy to receive fish. Uncle John came with my aunt and mother. He laid a huge sack at my feet. "Boy good. Worked hard," he said and patted my fanny. It took three of us to haul my fish away.

As I left Kalihiwai, low waves washed the shore. There were two sets of float lines bobbing in the sea. I prayed I could come back and enjoy the end of the *hukilau*.

* * *

A week went by without news. No matter, it was summer time. The ocean
sparkled with sunshine during the day. The evenings filled with gentle
breezes swaying the palm trees, and the moon casting a silver path across
the ocean to our home. We lived within the allure of the tropics which
induced an apathy that made me say, "I'll do it tomorrow."

Excitement blew away the laziness when a call came, "Come to Kalihiwai." Strange, the request was made in mid-afternoon, but I wasn't complaining, for I guessed I would be coming for the end of the *hukilau*.

Our auto, laden with food and goodies, motored downhill into the bay. I saw drying fish nets laid out on long poles and smoke rising from the ground in the center of the valley. People bustled about the beach. A great stack of driftwood stood beyond the pine trees. Leaving our car, I smelled cooked *kalua* pig, teriyaki meat, chicken *heka*, fried fish, and other delightful things to eat.

It was party time for all the people who had worked on the net pulling. News spread that eighty-five tons of fish had been sold. It was a special night for the polyglot of nationalities that composed Kaua'i. We joined together in friendship, drawn to Kalihiwai by the successful outcome of a community event, the *hukilau*.

The bonfire blazed into light, jetting yellow-orange flames into the sky. Someone strummed a guitar, a ukulele chimed in, and a steel bass played. Everyone sang Hawaiian songs, *"Ahi wela, mai nei loco. I ka hana a ke aloha. E lalawe ne'i ku'u kino...."* With a full belly and joyful music ringing in my ears, I fell asleep.

* * *

I must confess that what I have related is a composite of successful *hukilau*. I chose the most interesting aspects of each that I participated in to weave the story. As for the Hawaiian song, it is not a lullaby. It is a ribald recitation of the excitement of love: "There is a fire inside me. In the act of love, it overwhelms my body."

CHAPTER 15

Entrepreneurs

"Hawaiians have no land. They gave it away for nothing," my mother said. She went on to remind me, "Never sell land. Leave for your children."

My dad as a pioneer showman traveled the islands showing his movies at plantation labor camps. He couldn't afford to buy land. When he needed a tent or a hall he rented it. "Renting is not good," he said. "Someone else owns the property and can kick you out."

My grandfather understood the importance of owning land. When he arrived on Kaua'i to work at Kilauea Sugar Plantation, he bought acreage from a Hawaiian, built a home, and started a farm. But he lost it and his supervisor's job because he filed a lawsuit against the plantation over water rights.

A little historical background is necessary to understand these tales that the elders related to me. When Captain Cook arrived in 1778, Hawai'i was a communal society. Land could not be owned, for it is a living thing that provides for the people. Germs brought by the foreigners decimated the Hawaiians. So many commoners died from measles, mumps, and other diseases that the intricate farming system of the islands fell apart. Destitution of his people caused the third king of Hawai'i to divide the land and institute the concept of private property. Missionary advisors had counseled the

king that land ownership would allow poor Hawaiians to develop farms,
build homes, and escape poverty.

Over the course of the nineteenth century, the Hawaiian failed to understand the legal requirements to secure land. Foreigners who came to the Islands understood the process of acquiring private property. By the time of the Spanish-American War, almost half of Hawai'i was owned by a few entities. The plantations were the most aggressive land acquirers and since sugar cane needs lots of water, they made certain that they controlled the rivers and streams. Barring people from access to water is contrary to Hawaiian tradition.

On annexation, the United States received the former monarchy lands in trust from the Republic of Hawai'i, approximately forty percent of Hawai'i. The new Territory controlled the remaining government land.

Kapa'a was territorial land. The new government divided it into parcels and allowed citizens to acquire lots to build homesteads. Non-citizens could not acquire lots. This rule excluded many Chinese, Japanese, and others from acquiring land. The result: plots of ground became vested in wives or children who were citizens of the Territory.

In the old days welfare did not exist, nor was any social safety net in place to save ordinary people from penury. My dad lived on the edge of bankruptcy. Whenever I asked, "Can I have a nickel?" His answer, "I'm broke ass."

I understood his meaning since I grew up in the Depression years. Besides, his credo was, "The only good boy is a hard working boy that doesn't ask for money." This is a maxim his father preached and Dad believed that a child should grow up a penny pincher.

A landless part-Hawaiian, Dad convinced Mother that land should be bought to build a movie house. But persuading a wife was not as difficult as asking a Big Five Company to part with land.

It took several visits to American Factors in Lihue and promises that the use of the purchased acre would be for a theater providing "wholesome entertainment" before a deal was struck. After the transaction the family left without me and lived in America for two years, studying movie theaters and equipment.

They returned in mid-1939 to begin construction of the largest movie house in the islands, the Roxy Theater, a three-story structure seating one thousand and fifty. It was a magnificent building with a large stage sufficient to hold an orchestra and dancers. Its sound equipment was state of the art. Carbon projectors lit up a huge silver screen, making the players bigger than life. Red velvet curtains, art deco paintings, and exquisite furnishings graced the theater with an elegance that had never been seen on Kaua'i.

My father was a brave Hawaiian. To fulfill his dream of land owner-ship, he mortgaged himself to the hilt. It was an action that had cost other Hawaiians dearly when they could not pay what they owed. But as he said, "Nothing ventured, nothing gained."

His words are prophetic, for when you analyze the foundations of Kapa'a town, you realize that adventurers saw opportunity in the mud flats that wealthy sugar planters did not. Kapa'a in early times was bounded by marshland, streams, and the sea. It was not the best area for raising the staple crop of the common people, taro, or for growing sugar cane.

Wong Aliou, a Chinese immigrant, saw rice-growing opportunity in the swamps of Kapa'a. He became wealthy through growing and selling rice. With his earnings he bought land and became the prime owner of property in the town. Unfortunately, during the boom years of rice grow-ing, Hawaiians did not take advantage of this, despite the fact that taro fields and rice paddies have striking similarities.

Polynesian colonizers brought sugar cane with them to use for thatch-ing huts and as a wind break. It was the Chinese and then Caucasians who saw the opportunity to become wealthy by grinding cane into molasses and producing sugar. For these entrepreneurs the ownership of vast land areas was a necessary corollary to wealth. Hawaiian plantation workers never became owners of sugar mills. The only Hawaiian to make the attempt was King David Kalakaua who came to Kapa'a in 1876, built a sugar mill, and planted cane in the foothills. Despite having control of cheap land, his venture failed and he abandoned his mill.

In 1900, rice was the second largest export from Hawai'i. Twenty years later competition and a shrinking market eliminated it as an export. But pineapple, indigenous to South America, replaced rice. James Dole made Hawai'i the pineapple Mecca of the world, planting fields of the golden fruit and building canneries to process them.

Retired plantation workers from Asia saw a chance to gain wealth in growing pineapple for sale. Several became pineapple farmers on landhold-ings near Kapa'a where they serviced an independently owned cannery and prospered. But Hawaiians were not learned in raising pineapple. They understood growing taro and swine.

It was rare indeed for any person in the Hawai'i of the 1930s to accumulate wealth unless they owned land. Few Hawaiians did. Many of those who I grew up with were landless, scratching out a bare existence. It was audacious for my Hawaiian parents to pursue a dream of land ownership to build a business that might lead them to prosperity.

* * *

Roxy Theater in New York was called the "Cathedral of the Motion Pictures." Its six thousand seats made it the largest theater in the world. Movies, stage shows, and a precision dance team, the "Roxyettes," were its weekly bill of fare. This grand movie house provided the inspiration for Dad to dream big.

Excitement sparked Kapa'a on opening night, November 18, 1939. Our theater was packed. A first rate movie was featured and after the show, a full orchestra with "popular local talent" entertained. Plus door prizes were given away. A well-dressed crowd attended that first show. Even the ushers looked up-scale New York, wearing white shirts, bow ties, dark pants, and shoes, unusual for a laid-back slipper-wearing community.

The design of the theater was not just for movies, but, like its inspiration, to have dance groups and entertainers perform on a large stage. The world of "The Big Apple" had been brought to our isolated island.

Special artists performed at the Roxy. I still recall the night when the two-story-high red velvet curtains parted. On an ebony stage, a black contralto, framed by a massive silver screen, took the opening applause of a packed house. I rested my forearms on the brown railing of the second-floor balcony seats studying the singer who had traveled from the East Coast of the United States to thrill our audience of disparate races.

Marian Anderson's appearance brought home to us in Hawai'i the ugliness of prejudice that existed on the American Continent. A few months earlier the famous singer had been banned from Constitution Hall in Washington D.C. by the Daughters of the American Revolution. President

Roosevelt and his wife Eleanor, in response to this racial insult, scheduled an open air concert at the Lincoln Memorial, attended by 75,000 people.

Anderson sang spirituals at our theater, but, more important, she made us aware of the plight of black people in America. Without the capacity of the Roxy to provide a fitting stage for such a world figure, her message would not have resonated to us.

Watching her performance, I thought of the meaning of the Civil War, the issues that divided the Union, and the aftermath of Southern defeat. Although a voracious reader, I had not given American History much consideration as I preferred books of fantasy and fiction. Her presence turned me to learning about our country's past and events occurring in distant parts of the world.

When German tanks and Stuka dive bombers plunged into Poland, the sounds of war shook the theater. Everything displayed on the big screen was awe-inspiring. Pathe News and *The March of Time* brought home to me the horrors of blitzkrieg in Europe. And in the Pacific there came news of the sinking of the American gunboat Panay, the Japanese invasion of China, and the rape of Nanking.

This jolted me from my myopic interest in fantasy and turned my attention to world events. Despite reading as much as I could about the new type of lightning warfare, and the brutality of the battles in China, nothing in books equaled the powerful impact of the reality displayed on the silver screen.

Despite this newfound knowledge, events occurring across the seas seemed remote to the people of our island. A broad ocean formed an insurmountable barrier to war. The airplane is simply a flying boat that takes off and lands in the water and cannot fly very far. These were the aircraft I saw flying between the islands. I had no idea that carriers could transport airplanes thousands of miles over the sea and attack us. The American military and Hawai'i soon learned the reality of modern warfare. There would be nowhere on earth that was safe.

CHAPTER 16

Ko'olau The Leper

"He hid near that waterfall," Jack pointed. "Fifty soldiers came up the hill to get him, but Ko'olau picked them off until they ran back to the beach. See the white scars on the sides of the valley? The frightened militia shot artillery shells all over Kalalau trying to kill him."

Cawing frigate birds soared over deep clefts in the Na Pali coast. Clouds that shrouded sight on our arrival had evaporated, leaving only wisps of white drifting along the peaks. The ocean from the shore to the horizon glowed deep blue with thousands of white caps dancing towards us, lifting up and collapsing as the wind rose and faded. Ferns, shrubs, grass, trees, flowers grew in verdant green along the ridges adding a wild jungle effect to the primitive beauty of Kalalau Valley.

"Why did the soldiers want to kill him?"

"Long story. You've heard of the *mai Pake*?"

"I think so."

"It is leprosy, a disease that kills your nerves and causes your body to rot and parts of it to fall off."

"That's the Chinese sickness?"

Jack nodded. "Long time ago, the *mai* hit Hawaiians hard. The *haoles* forced those with the disease to be imprisoned in Kalaupapa. Hard place to survive in," Jack added, bitterness in his voice. He stopped talking. His eyes misted.

"What's wrong?"

"My brother was taken to that place on the northern coast of Moloka'i. High cliffs on one end of flat land and wild ocean on the other. No escape."

An idea struck me. "Kaua'i lepers who didn't want to go to Kalaupapa came here."

"Yes, maybe one hundred-fifty people fled to this valley, built homes, planted taro, and lived in the old fashioned way."

"Was Ko'olau one of them?"

"He didn't come right away. He wanted to live in Waimea with his wife and son. A doctor discovered he had the *mai* and said, 'You must go to the leper colony but your wife can't go with you.' Ko'olau answered, 'God put us together, and men cannot part us.' The family left for Kalalau."

"Why didn't they leave him alone?"

"'He is a law breaker', the *haoles* said. Sheriff came. They had a gun-fight. Sheriff died. Soldiers came to get him and all the other lepers, but Ko'olau is a crack shot."

"Did he die?"

Jack smiled, "We all die, but the soldiers never got him."

I was silent for a few moments, thinking. It was a sad story of the mal-treatment of Hawaiians. Provision was not made by the Health Department for the feeding and caring of the afflicted. Dumped into the ocean off Molokai, they swam ashore and cared for themselves.

"Lepers in Kalalau not hurting anybody. Why not leave them alone?"

"I say like you, but this is *haole* justice. Lepers are law breakers, must go to Moloka'i. So their village was burned and everybody shipped to Kalaupapa."

"Making Kalalau a scary place, where only dead people live," I added.

Driving away from the valley, I thought of the sin of being Hawaiian. My parents, who were fluent in the language and raised in the old ways, were ashamed of their color and did not teach us Hawaiian. Public schools banned its use. There was a suggestion that native people were lazy and inferior in intellect. Unfortunately, with my "do it tomorrow attitude," I added to this illusion.

These were weighty issues to ponder. At the time, I did not have an answer to the plight of the Hawaiian race. But as I thought more upon it, I realized that the ordinary plantation worker existed in a state of subjugation. They must obey the regulations laid down by the sugar people, not make trouble by unionizing, and making demands for higher wages and better working conditions.

We lived in a cocoon fabricated by the Big Five to ensure that the political, social, and economic conditions that they had created in Hawai'i were under their control. The news media touted Hawai'i as a tropical paradise, "The melting pot of the Pacific. Where races blended together living in harmony."

Despite this, there were elements of conflict smoldering under the surface. This festering of trouble resulted from the infliction of the deep wounds of discrimination, the unlawful overthrow of the Hawaiian Kingdom, the violent suppression of strikers, and the human pyramid with its broad base of impoverished people.

My thinking at the time was not as clear as I have just stated. But my visit to Kalalau Valley and the story of Ko'olau set in motion thoughts that there was something amiss in Hawai'i. I recalled the whispers of the unlawful overthrow of the Queen, of the protests against annexation to America, of the claim that "foreigner's take, take, take, and no give back."

There existed a hidden dissatisfaction among laborers regarding unfair treatment by those in power. Smoldering elements of future conflict lay waiting for the time to be set in motion against the system of plantation paternalism, a polite tyranny that controlled Hawai'i.

CHAPTER 17

The Rapture Of The Deep

An underwater canyon that stretches into darkness conjures evil things that slither from the void and strike. An island is a mountain of volcanic rock that has built up from the floor of the sea. Erupting lava breaks the surface of the ocean and continues to rise until the supply of molten rock is turned off when the hot spot in the earth moves away. Beneath the surface are valleys and ridges that mimic the mountains above the sea.

Swimming along an underwater arroyo, I was attracted by the multi-colored rocks, dark forests of coral, caves where fish swam in and out staring at me with lidless eyes. I sensed danger in the deep. It was like swimming into the womb and being enveloped by the remembrance of the peaceful-ness of my first home. This mesmerizing effect was dangerous. I wanted to go deeper and recapture the comfort of being within my mother.

Fortunately, I had no weights on my body to negate my buoyancy and without webbed feet, the attempt to kick deeper only produced pain in my ears. I backed away from the rapture of the deep despite seeing schools of big fish swimming along the sides of the descending canyon.

My friend Pete surfaced nearby.

"Big game," I said.

He shrugged and answered, "All we have are puny wire spears with blunt heads. Rubber sling shots with no power."

"Yeah, they are just good enough for whacking manini in a cave. Besides, my mom said not to go in deep water, too many sharks."

"Mama's boy?"

"No way, but since you're smart, you try fishing in that canyon."

Pete did not seize the gauntlet. Was he chicken? He gave me an answer after some moments.

"Our equipment is no good."

I knew he was right. How could you be a blue water hunter if all you had was a short wire spear and tight fitting goggles? You could not keep your face under water long enough to spot a big fish or be warned of an approaching shark. I thought of a picture in my history book of a two-dimensional ancient Egyptian standing on the shore hurling a sharp stick into the water. In four thousand years, we had not made any major advances in the art of spear fishing.

"Maybe we try using a net," Pete said.

Again an image popped into my head of a Roman fighter with a net and three-pronged spear battling another warrior dressed in armor holding a sword and shield. I backed away from the canyon and found myself in an area of sand ringed by coral. I felt like a gladiator in the coliseum. My surroundings made me realize that we were not equipped to fight or capture whatever might come from the dark void beyond us. And no doubt we must fight, for *mano* can smell the thrashing of the speared fish when it tries to break free. We didn't have an *ike jime*, kill spike, to dispatch the struggling animal or defend against the shark.

"We're a big joke," I said, breaking the surface and gulping air.

"What?" Pete answered.

"We are only good for manini, not the big stuff."

"Honolulu boys have good spears, better slings. I know some older guys who have them."

I dove underwater and grabbed a rock six feet below the surface. My lungs were stronger with constant diving, my asthmatic wheezes just a nuisance. No longer did I spend hours shivering in bed after spear fishing.

I looked at the beauty of the underwater world, the multi-colored tropical fish flitting from stone to stone, the sun piercing through translucent water and shining on a sea floor, of changing light like the neon signs at my father's theater. I wanted more adventure than what I found in shallow water. I wanted the challenges that the deep provided and the fear that I knew would come when *mano* arrived to steal my catch.

Floating to the surface, I called to Pete, "Where are these guys?"

* * *

Along the Kapa'a shoreline two blocks from the government road were a string of shanties where Hawaiians lived. It was easy to spot their homes. Nets would be spread out on poles, drying in the sun. Cars stood outside, rusting in the salt air.

Pete and I walked along the railroad tracks heading to the cannery where my mother had worked for many years. The manager, Mr. Horner, was a very nice man and a fair person that everyone liked.

When I mentioned this to Pete he said, "You know his big house on the corner of Wailua Bay?"

"Yeah, the white one sitting by the beach, lots of black rocks in front and heavy surf."

"True, but on a good day you go outside his place, good fishing."

"I hear plenty sharks outside."

"You want big fish? You got to go where the sharks are."

That was not appealing. It's hard enough to swim from a sand beach out to sea because of the huge waves pounding the shore. But leaping from a rocky headland into the ocean was dangerous. The ocean's constant smashing shoves you into the stones, forcing a scramble among the rocks to avoid injury. Re-approaching the launching point, surging water flings your body along the sharp coral, scraping your flesh. The receding wave thrusts you into deep water, only to fling you back. Once past the constant surge and into deep water, there could be sharks waiting. From them, there was no escape.

A train hauling cars laden with burnt cane stalks was some distance away as we balanced our way north on rails heated by the sun. The flat iron was warm on my bare feet. I wanted to fall off onto a railroad tie. But

I was engaged in a challenge match to walk on the rails to our destination, the shacks of Hawaiian fishermen. I spread my arms, balanced myself, and shuffled forward. Pete was ahead. I hurried. I didn't want him to win.

We approached the railroad bridge crossing over Waitala, a sinister pond where it was claimed Dracula lived. I had seen in its mud a wooden crate. It was said to be his coffin. Around a bend in the tracks, the sugar train puffed clouds of white steam. It sped toward the bridge. Pete crossed over. I was twenty feet from the trestle.

Could I make it before the train's cowcatcher smashed me? Waitala was darkest where the pillars of the bridge anchored into the sand bottom. Its sides were eight to ten feet straight up studded with projections of stone. If I could not get across in time I must leap from the bridge to escape the train. The sheerness of the compacted coral wall meant a swim in the murky water looking for a way out. Death would surely come from drowning or Dracula searching for my blood. But if I didn't cross, Pete would surely win.

I hurried along the rail, speeding for the bridge. Roaring in defiance, the steam engine charged toward me like a maddened bull, its course clearly outlined by the tracks that it rolled upon. Across the bridge Pete scurried to the side. I was near the trestle. A howling whistle warned me that the locomotive refused to stop for foolish children, especially since the engineer could not see me. I was two arms' lengths from the bridge. Should I cross? Only a second remained to make a decision. I could leap into Waitala if in danger. But what about Dracula? The word "Spalding" on the front shield of the steam engine filled my eyes.

At the edge of the bridge, I chose to lose to Pete and slid off the rail to safety. Train cars plunged past me, stuffed with cane. A smell of burnt leaves filled my lungs. Chains that imprisoned the stalks clashed together. Their clinking sounded like the clashing made by Frankenstein's monster as he fought against the iron links binding him to his prison cell. Watching the passage of the loaded wagons, all I could think about was that I had chickened out. I wondered if Pete would tell the other boys that I failed the challenge. Oh, what misery I would face as the teasing would dwell on my fear. But more important, I hoped word wouldn't get back to Mom of what we had done. I wouldn't be able to walk for a week.

The last car passed. Pete stood on the other side of the bridge. He smiled as I crossed over. When I reached him he said, "You did the smart thing." We put our arms around each other, walked between the rails, heading for the shacks of the spear fishermen.

CHAPTER 18

Rain

It rained through the entire movie until the island was awash with water. During the course of the on-screen storm, God-fearing minister Walter Huston tried to convince Sadie Thompson, played by Joan Crawford, to end her sinning and repent. Through an hour and a half of a motion picture, undoubtedly shot in a drenching downpour, Huston ranted about evil leading to the self-destruction of a wicked woman. When Sadie finally promised to change her ways, the married minister realized he wanted her to be sinful and make love to him. Huston committed suicide in the end.

I left the Roxy facing a deluge pouring onto Kaua'i. A tropical storm had moved over the island and black clouds masked the sun hiding Mount Wai'ale'ale. The primitive Territorial weather system had not predicted the severity of the storm, so none of us were prepared for the drenching we received.

Finally home after navigating through streets covered with water, I worried that, like the movie, the downpour wouldn't stop until something disastrous occurred. But a bright idea struck me. The flooding could lead to adventure. I scurried to Ambrose's house across from our home and said to him, "We go surfing."

"What you mean?" he answered.

"Streets covered with water, many yards have ponds round like cushions."

Ambrose got the idea. On our ironing boards, we propelled ourselves along the road skimming the flood fronting our homes. Pelted by rain, I felt glorious. When I fell from my board I landed in deep water and didn't get hurt.

"Ambrose, let's try your tin canoe."

We hauled it out of his garage, its dirt floor muddy with water. It was easy loading onto it. We stood on opposite sides of the vessel, one foot in the boat and the other resting on the lawn. On the cadence of one-two-three we pushed off, settled in the canoe, and paddled.

But we paid a price for pelting rain. "We filling up, bail," Ambrose said.

I used a can to toss out water from the boat and realized it had a leak. "This thing got a crack in the bottom,"

"Use your hands."

"Better when it gets full, we get out and turn it over."

My suggestion made sense and we both pushed hard on our ti-leaf shaped paddles, propelling our slowly filling craft down the street. Suddenly we were under attack. A tin canoe, painted with a Germanic cross, shot out from behind a hedge aiming for us.

"Archibald and Ivan are going to ram," I yelled.

Ambrose steered our boat away, as the craft of the two Russian wild men slid by. "You guys declaring war," Ambrose yelled.

"Yeah," answered Ivan, whom we dubbed "The Terrible" because he was crazy. He and his brother ran around the neighborhood with capes, wooden swords, and garbage can shields and challenged you to duels. The boys claimed they were "White Russians" who had fled that country. When I first met them, this claim didn't make sense since I thought all Russians were white. It was explained to me that the family had been loyal to the Tsar and forced to flee Russia when the Communists took over. They escaped from Siberia and lived in China before traveling to Hawai'i. "Followers of the Tsar are called 'White Russians,'" Ivan had said.

Whether we wanted to or not, Ambrose and I were in for it. The two boys were relentless in their aggression. They were not mean, but rough guys who liked to mix it up, which soon became abundantly clear as they paddled their canoe into a ramming position. Our craft was awash in water and slow. Theirs was nimble.

"Ramming speed," Ivan yelled and the Russian craft lumbered toward us. Rain came in buckets. I heard a dull "clunk" as the enemy craft hit our boat. Ivan began pounding away with a wet rag mop like a berserk Fuzzy Wuzzy from the movie, *Four Feathers*.

"Can't see too good," Ambrose said.

We were blinded by rain. Ivan's weapon banged against our canoe. We retaliated with our wooden paddles. But the downpour was too much as water filled both vessels and they grounded onto the macadamized road.

"Abandon ship," I yelled, scraping my leg on the edge of the tin as I hustled from our canoe.

Archibald came at me. I avoided him as his attempt to tackle went awry and he plunged head first into the water. Ambrose, who was bigger than me and a wild guy himself, was hand wrestling with Ivan when thunder struck. The boom was so powerful my ears hurt from the shattering sound.

All combat stopped from the shock of the explosion followed by more and more thunderous rumbles.

"You get inside right now," Ivan's mother shrieked from a hedge.

At sea, jagged shafts of lightning plunged from the overcast sky into the ocean. Our tin canoes were ungrounded metal targets for Thor's bolts.

The war ended with sunken canoes abandoned and kids slogging through the rapidly rising water for home. You ask, "Where were my parents?"

They were at the Roxy trying to save the theater. My older sister was responsible for me, but she didn't know I was playing outside.

* * *

Kaua'i is known for having the wettest spot on earth, Wai'ale'ale Mountain. Clouds floating across the Pacific must rise to overcome its mile of height. The result is lots of rain. My island is called the "Garden Island" because of the lush tropical jungles caused by the incessant downpour upon this dormant volcano.

Unfortunately, the west side of Kapa'a has a wide crescent of marshland created by trapped water. The storm I have described deluged Kaua'i. The swamps became a lake. As the days passed water flooded the land and in some areas joined with the ocean.

My parents gave up trying to sandbag the Roxy. Flood waters poured into the ground floor, turning the theater into a swimming pool. Automobiles could not drive on the streets. The only means of travel was by boat.

When the rains reduced their ferocity, an exploration crew rowed into the theater. They reported that all seats on the ground floor were underwater. The stair rugs were soaked and needed replacement. Amazingly, the tin roof held up and only minor damage occurred to the ceiling.

For me it was a golden opportunity to catch fish. The melding together of fresh storm water with the sea had caused ocean fish to swim into the streets of Kapa'a and Waipouli. They soon suffered from lack of oxygen and swam dizzily along the roadway, moving in short spurts then stopping. You could see their gills bellowing as they tried to take in life-giving sea water.

"Ambrose," I said, "nenue coming right for you," pointing to a fish swimming slowly along the street. My pal reached, grabbed, and squeezed his hands shut, trapping the flat, silver ocean fish between his fingers. The animal flapped a little then stopped squirming.

"You think this guy sick?"

"Maybe, but this is ocean fish, he cannot live in brackish water."

Both of us were oblivious to the severe damage that had been wrought by the storm. Businesses were ruined by water. Could the Roxy survive? Seats needed to be removed and dried. Soggy carpets had to be replaced. Interior walls would need repainting. With substantial mortgage debt, our family faced hard times. I could see why the plantations had abandoned the low land of Kapa'a and chose to plant sugar cane on the higher ground above it. The only good news was that no one died in the flooding.

Rain finally stopped and the high water receded into a muddy ocean. Dead fish were everywhere, unable to swim back to their natural habitat. I thought of the movie and wondered whether our life would change as a result of this natural disaster. Bible thumping, wages of sin, preacher Walter Huston succumbed to the sins of lust and adultery. He paid the price for his hypocrisy, winding up as food for the fishes.

Had my parents sinned by trying to accomplish too much with too little? Like the islands in the movies *Rain* and *The Hurricane*, we were at the mercy of wind, rain, and sea. Could we who are Hawaiian overcome God's challenges or are we doomed to be impoverished?

CHAPTER 19

Whispers Of War

Machine gun bullets sprayed through barbed wire in no-man's land. Explosions rocked the theater. German artillery blasted the American trenches. A hand grenade tumbled into the shell hole where soldiers of the "Fighting 69th" huddled. Jimmy Cagney, a coward, seized a doughboy's helmet, using it and his body to smother the explosive. He died in the arms of Father Duffy, receiving absolution for his past sins.

Pathe News sensationalized the battles going on in Europe with tragic pictures of London on fire. *The Great Dictator*, a political movie, depicted a man with a Charlie Chaplin moustache terrorizing innocent people, especially a race named the Jews. All of it was unreal like a dream. No one could possibly be interested in our islands. What was there to conquer, sugar cane, pineapple? We had nothing of value like iron or oil. So why show these propaganda movies?

I think that Washington D.C. and the film companies were preparing America for war. Our isolationism meant that no one wanted to fight. Even patriotic Irving Berlin songs could not get us to march "Over There."

Soldiers did not defend Kaua'i or any of the islands outside of Oahu. If war came, we were lost, as easy to take as it had been for the United States to seize Hawaii fifty years before. But why worry? America was not concerned. Our islands were a sleepy, backward place, far away from the hot spots exploding in Europe and Asia.

As Hitler's armies plunged into Yugoslavia, the theater was patched together and after repairs we showed movies again. But the audiences were sparse and I could see the lines of worry on the faces of my parents.

The combat movies had one salutary effect: my friend Sooky and I bought firecrackers and set up mock battles with our tin soldiers. These toys had made an appearance on Kaua'i just as the movies became warlike. It was great fun burying small explosives in the sand and, as enemy infantry charged, lighting a fuse and watching the explosion. Sometimes we would throw a lighted cracker into a defended fort or occupied trench. That was dangerous, especially if the fuse burned fast and the fireworks exploded in your hand.

We didn't think of the enemy tin soldiers as Japanese or German. They were just the bad guys like when we played Cowboys and Indians with the Japanese boys in the neighborhood. Interestingly, the Nisei kids did not want to "waste time" blowing up tin soldiers.

When German tanks blitzkrieged into Russia, I overheard Dad say, "I can't meet the payroll." After that, my sister and I became ushers in the theater. My father scolded us for wasting food and kept telling Mom, "Pinch every penny."

While Hitler gloated over his stunning victories in the East, things got worse for our family. The bank threatened foreclosure of the Roxy property. The meaning of these events were somewhat lost on me. Russia was so far away that I could not see its relevance to our lives. What did foreclosure mean?

What about Japan? What about it? Our island was almost half Japanese. There were Japanese-language schools spread across Kaua'i and on occasion I had gone into a classroom. Prominently displayed was the picture of the Emperor surrounded by rising sun flags. I had many Japanese friends and spent many hours at their homes. There was nothing sinister in being with them and in no way did I feel threatened.

Of course, there is a foreclosure to be concerned about. But our extended family had always struggled through dire economic times. Somehow we had made it. For a Hawaiian family there was always the sea to fall back on.

A summer that was dark and threatening for the rest of the world was glorious for me. Pete and I met the Hawaiian men, one of them was Jack.

They were in the midst of dividing scores of big fish they had speared. We begged to join them in their next foray into the deep, but they did not want the responsibility of caring for kids.

I was lucky, for Jack gave me a sleek five-foot spring steel spear with a shining metal barb that folded onto the pointed end of the shaft. "This is my *kini*," I said as I thanked him for the marvelous gift. For those of you who might not understand the word, *kini* was a favorite marble, a sure winner in every game.

Armed with my *kini* I learned the real art of spear fishing, stalking an elusive quarry, taking a deep breath, diving, drawing back the spear with its rubber propellant, and firing. Many misses at first, but when I finally hit a good sized fish a wild struggle ensued when the animal fled with my spear. I moved *wiki wiki* before it dove into a hole. When I secured the big fish, I knew I had moved from a manini catcher to the next level, an open water spear fisherman. Still to be attained was the status of a blue water hunter and the inevitable encounters with mano. It is a goal that I did not achieve during the glorious summer of 1941.

* * *

"Bank has started foreclosure," Dad said. "I'm broke again."

"I'll go back to work in the cannery," Mom answered.

I understood the despondency he felt. Over the years we had many conversations about his early life. At eight years he was snatched from his Mau'i home by his father to work at the Parker ranch on the Big Island, packing mail from the ranch to Hilo. A runaway at fifteen, he had arrived in Honolulu during the tumultuous time following the overthrow of the Hawaiian Kingdom. Desperate to improve himself, he worked at any job and went to school. With increased learning he took correspondence courses in business while serving as a mounted patrolman for the new Territory of Hawai'i. He was capable at that job for he was part white and spoke fluent Hawaiian, a combination that allowed him to deal effectively with Caucasians and the native population.

Giving up his police job, my father turned to business. He operated a stage coach line, tried to be a fish monger, and opened a haberdashery store. His enterprises were failures for one simple reason, "Too much on the cuff and too little in the till."

"Movie business is the best. You pay your nickel at the door or you don't get in. No credit, just cash on the line." This influenced him to become a silent movie operator, plus the multi-cultural audiences who came to the show not understanding a word of English. Pantomime, the art of Marcel Marceau, is a universal language that can be understood by anyone. He believed he could show silent movies anywhere.

Dad learned the business and, once proficient, decided to become "the showman of the Pacific." He loaded his equipment on a wagon and began touring the islands showing his films in labor camps and towns. After the Great War, he took silent movies to Japan, China, Thailand, and the Philippines.

Dad settled in Kapa'a where he saw opportunity. It was my mother's home. For a decade, he was successful with a small theater, the Rialto. But he wanted to build and own his dream and he had. But now in the fall of 1941, his three-story, thousand-fifty-seat Roxy was doomed. "Fernandez's folly," people whispered. "Theater is too big." What they said appeared to be true. We were in a recession with very few customers.

* * *

My parents bought a Philco radio shaped like a tombstone with the face of a clown. The only stations we could get were in Honolulu. The radio was AM only and did not have shortwave. We used the radio for news and on Sundays for the special shows.

It is amazing how my sister and I eagerly waited for Sunday to come when we could listen to *The Shadow* or *The Inner Sanctum*. As the voices of the players became terrified and the background music foreboding, I pressed my ear to the little brown box trying to catch every word. That's when the arguments came as my sister whined, "You're too close, I want to listen too."

"Not so."

"You are too."

Higher authority would order me from the set and I often missed the culminating moment of horror. Sometimes when I was sick, I listened for an hour to other shows like *Oxydol's Ma Perkins,* something innocent and wholesome.

We lived in a cocoon. The radio lulled us into a false sense of security. No talk shows alerted us to significant news of the world. We heard no commentators discussing President Roosevelt's embargo on Japan or his ultimatum to the Empire to leave China. These were acts of war. But none of us knew about them. The authorities knew of these militant demands but did not prepare us for war.

Thanksgiving was celebrated with duck from our farm. But as we sat around the dinner table, I felt a sense of gloom. Not about world events, but because of the impending loss of my parents' hopes and dreams, Roxy Theater.

Part Two

W A R

I dedicate this portion of my book to the
courageous and loyal Nisei men of the 100th Battalion,
442d Regimental Combat Team of the United States Army,
and the Military Intelligence Service

MaiKai!

CHAPTER 20

War

It bloomed a glorious day. Sunbeams painted the horizon golden. Clouds were absent. The sky was royal blue. I sat in the back of the family truck watching slow waves roll onto Kapa'a beach, the breeze so gentle they weren't capped in foam. I listened to the soothing rustle of coconut leaves as we motored by the town park.

At church, the tedium resulting from an early morning mass was replaced by the excitement building inside me. This was a perfect day for spear fishing.

Our Dodge truck rolled into the sand driveway. Someone said, "Turn on the radio."

It was 8:15 a.m., Sunday, December 7, 1941. The Philco speaker screeched, "We are under attack. The Japanese are bombing Pearl Harbor. We are going off the air." The radio went static.

This had to be a joke? Scampering to the street, I searched in the direction of Honolulu, seeking the airplanes buzzing around Oahu.

My mother screamed, "Get inside."

"Mom, it's too far away to hurt me."

"You get inside," my father ordered.

Reluctantly, I marched back in, thinking the worst place to be in an air raid, was in a house. Hadn't they seen all those war movies of Warsaw, Amsterdam, and London with buildings on fire from aerial bombing?

I could not deny that there was fright on Mom's face. Her phone calls for information provided only one answer, "We are at war with Japan. Stay home."

Our survival prospects were bleak. Kaua'i did not have regular army soldiers protecting it. Pearl Harbor and Oahu were more important, all military resources concentrated there to make it what the military called "the strongest fortress in the world."

Earlier in the year, the Hawai'i National Guard had been activated to protect the islands. A battalion of its 299th Infantry Regiment had been assigned to Kaua'i. How do I know this? Friend Jack who was sweet on my cousin, Alice, had been called up for active duty in the 299th. His unit had two 75mm cannon to defend the island. Added to this, many of the recruits were Nisei, Japanese-American citizens. It was not a secret that the U.S. military questioned the loyalty of the Japanese in Hawai'i, fearing sabotage, espionage, and a general uprising if there was an invasion by soldiers of the Empire of the Rising Sun.

There were many things to be fearful of on this first day of war, but in my heart I could not believe that men I had grown up with, played with, and worked beside, would turn against me and my family. This faith would be tested in the days to come.

December 7th continued on its dreary pace hour after hour without news of the results of the attack on Pearl Harbor. The Governor's declaration of martial law suspended our rights, closed the civil courts, and handed over all power to the U.S. military. They banned automobiles from the highways, ships from the sea, imposed a blackout starting at 6:00 p.m., and a curfew. We were no longer sleepy, laid back Hawai'i, but a military camp where breaking the rules meant immediate punishment without trial.

From my bedroom window, I stared at a calm ocean, darkening as twilight passed to night. Were enemy ships coming? We had nothing to defend us should there be an invasion. Would my Nisei friends be loyal to America? This jumble of thoughts had to be a bad dream. It had to be a nightmare that would be over when I woke up. But the reality of war came to me with the darkness that spread over the island. Lights did not wink on from neighboring houses. Except for the barking of a dog and the crash of the surf there was silence. Huddled in our home, the family spoke in whispers, fearing to be heard by something evil.

With nothing to do, no radio to listen to or movie to see, I placed my toy soldiers on the window sill facing the sea and put my BB gun under the bed. I shivered as I pulled my sheet over my head to hide from the enemy and wondered if tomorrow I would be a prisoner of Japan.

* * *

Bleak days followed, made worse by a tropical storm that struck the islands after the attack. There were no incidents on Kaua'i, although Filipinos angered by enemy air attacks in the Philippines patrolled the streets during the day with cane knives. My Japanese friends did not come out to play, for there was an uncertainty as to how they might be treated by those in authority. Rumors of their relocation to some remote area began to circulate. The language school at the edge of Kapa'a was shut down, the picture of the Emperor removed, and the teachers taken into custody.

We were at war with Germany, Japan, and Italy. These nations appeared all-powerful, for the Nazis had conquered Europe and the Japanese were raising havoc in the Far East. The only bright spot was the defense of Wake Island by four hundred Marines. They had beaten back a Japanese attack on December 11, inflicting heavy losses on enemy ships and men.

But this was the only cheerful news, because Japanese submarines had embargoed West Coast shipping and we faced starvation in Hawai'i. Eighty-five percent of food supplies for Oahu came from California. Although Kaua'i could make do for itself, the war effort required that Honolulu be supplied. Strict rationing was imposed. Since we had a farm below the Sleeping Giant Mountain, we got a little extra gas to do our agricultural work, but a movie house was not considered essential and no additional allotment was made to service it.

In those early days of the war, no one went to the movies. School was suspended. Public gatherings were banned. An information blackout imposed by the military leaked heroic news like the sacrifice of Collin P, Kelley and the defense of Wake Island. We prayed that the Marines would hold out over the overwhelming power of Japan.

One bright moment occurred in an otherwise dismal Christmas season. On Ni'ihau, an island twenty miles from Kaua'i, a Japanese pilot landed his Mitsubishi fighter plane and had been killed by Ben Kanahele. A Hawaiian had defeated a Japanese takeover of the Forbidden Island. The good news was tempered by sinister overtones: Nisei from Kapa'a had joined with the pilot to take control of the island and died in the fighting. To put the event in proper perspective, the saga of the battle for Ni'ihau needs to be told from the standpoint of what we know today before we relate the rumors and hearsay that swirled around Kaua'i in December of 1941.

After attacking Pearl Harbor, twenty-two-year-old Nishikaichi headed back to his carrier with six other aircraft. They were pounced upon by several Curtiss Hawk fighter planes. Superior in every aspect of aerial combat, the Zeros shot down the Americans. But Nishikaichi's gas tank was punctured. He could not make it back to his ship. Before the early morning strike on Pearl Harbor, Japanese pilots had been briefed to "head for uninhabited Ni'ihau" if their aircraft suffered damage. A submarine would pick them up.

Unknown to the Japanese, the island was occupied by three hundred pure Hawaiians. The Robinson family had owned the island since 1864 when they purchased it from the Hawaiian monarchy for ten thousand dollars.

Crash landing on Ni'ihau, the dazed pilot was pulled from his craft by a Hawaiian named Kaleohano who took his pistol and papers. The Hawaiian had no knowledge of the war that had started. Kaleohano brought in a Japanese alien beekeeper named Shintano to interpret. Shintano did not reveal that the Japanese had attacked Pearl Harbor.

The next day, Nishikaichi was treated as an honored guest with a luau given in celebration of his coming. At the merry party, he played a guitar and sang Japanese songs. This was the Hawai'i of the old days, tolerant and friendly to all. But someone listening to a radio broadcast learned of the war and the pilot was placed under house arrest.

Yoshio Harada, an American citizen working on Ni'ihau and born in Kapa'a, visited the pilot. Nishikaichi convinced him that "America is weak and Japan will win the war." Harada broke into a locker at the Robinson estate and stole a pistol and shotgun. He freed the pilot and the two men began three days of terror on Ni'ihau. They dismounted the Zero's machine guns and shot up the village, sending all the Hawaiians into hiding.

Kaleohano and five other men escaped and rowed to Kaua'i to alert the Robinsons of the invasion. On December 12-13 an expeditionary force of National Guardsmen were dispatched to the island.

Meanwhile, the two Japanese sought the pilot's papers taken by Kaleohano. They went to his home, searched it, and burnt it to the ground. Hawaiians who were foolish enough to return to the village for food were made prisoner. One of them was the wife of Ben Kanahele.

Ben was a sheep herder and known for his strength, able to lift one-hundred-and-fifty- pound sheep and load them on board ship for transport to Kaua'i. He had been alerted of trouble in the village and with his wife had gone there for food and to provide help.

Seeking to rescue his imprisoned wife and end the terrorism, Ben confronted the two Japanese. Nishikaichi shot Kanahele three times as the Hawaiian tried to end the terrorism. Ben later said, "After the third shot I got mad." Like a sheep, Kanahele picked up the pilot and dashed him against a stone wall. His wife proceeded to crush his skull with a stone. Harada shot himself in the stomach.

The battle of Ni'ihau ended. For helping the pilot, Irene Harada, a citizen of America, went to prison. Failing to disclose what he knew from his interviews with Nishikaichi, Shintano was interned on the U.S. mainland. Ben Kanahele received the Medal of Merit and Purple Heart. Nishikaichi became a war hero in his home town in Japan.

In December of 1941 the events that occurred on Ni'ihau became distorted by rumor and conjecture. We were proud of Kanahele for being a Hawaiian hero. But the knowledge that three Japanese, two of them citizens, had turned against America created fear and anger among those who distrusted Japanese-Americans. Rumors of reprisals and actions to imprison the huge population of Japanese on Kaua'i began to circulate. Speculation ran wild as to the reason the Japanese pilot had landed on Ni'ihau. In the 1930s some officers in the U.S. military and the Robinson family believed that if the Japanese attacked, they would conquer one of the outer islands to use as an air base. Was Nishikaichi an advance scout for a future invasion force?

News filtered to us that President Roosevelt wanted all Japanese removed from Oahu and imprisoned on Molokai or shipped to the continent. An order came from The Joint Chiefs of Staff to intern Japanese-Americans "as soon as possible."

At gunpoint, Nisei soldiers in the Hawaiian National Guard were ordered to surrender their weapons and discharged from service. They faced internment as well. Eventually, to solve the issue of disloyalty, all former Japanese-American soldiers in Hawai'i were shipped to the U.S. mainland and formed into the 100th Infantry Battalion.

Although there were no other incidents of defection by Japanese-American citizens or espionage in Hawai'i, serious damage had been done to the cause of freedom by the events on Ni'ihau. In December as Japanese submarines sank ships, made surface attacks on island facilities, and launched incendiary raids, fear and hysteria grew. This angst infected the Western United States and led to Roosevelt's internment order for all Japanese on the Pacific Coast. One hundred and ten thousand American citizens were thrust into concentration camps in the interior of the U.S. Eighteen hundred came from Hawai'i.

* * *

When Ben Kanahele's picture appeared in the *Garden Island* and his heroism headlined, morale on Kaua'i soared, for up to that point, the news of the war had been shocking. Two British battleships had been sunk by airpower and Japan was invading the Philippines.

I sought out my friend Sooky to tell him the news. "Look at the paper," I said, "Hawaiian guy real strong. He picked up Japanese guy like sheep and threw him against a stone wall."

"I know all about it," Sooky said.

"Let's prepare for battle in case of invasion."

"Like what?"

"We can build a fort. You get your BB gun, I'll get mine and we'll defend it."

Sooky agreed and we went to the beach less than fifty yards from our homes. There was a stand of pine trees fronting the ocean and the sand on the seaside of the coast line slanted towards the water. We proceeded to dig until we hit ocean. We banked the walls of the fort with wet sand to make it firm. With our defensive position completed, we squirreled into it with our BB guns resting on niches in the front parapet.

Searching the horizon, I said, "Do you think the Japanese will invade Kaua'i?"

"They bombed Pearl Harbor, landed on Ni'ihau, why not?" Sooky answered.

"We'll shoot them if they come," I said, firing my BB gun. The tiny brass bullet plopped into the lagoon. Its plunge created a ripple in the slowly moving water. I began to wonder if what we were doing was a good idea.

"American ships cannot come here. They are scared of the submarines. Maybe we will starve," Sooky said, a sad look in his eyes.

"We have a farm beneath Sleeping Giant. Got ducks and chickens in our yard, don't worry, we can make it."

"But if the Japanese come, they will take everything. Where can we hide? No place to go, mountains everywhere."

"We'll hide in the hills."

"Bad. Lost tribe lives in the center of the island, they will eat us. Maybe you have Hawaiian gods that can help?" Sooky said, then remembered God's commandment about false gods coming before him. "I'm sorry I said that. It's a mortal sin."

"My family is raised Catholic too, but my mother believes in the *aumakua*, the personal god who can protect you. Maybe I can ask her for help from the *akua*."

"Mortal sin to even talk about it," Sooky wailed.

"All right, if we can't get help from the *aumakua* and God won't help us then…"

"Sin, sin, you took the Lord's name in vain."

"I didn't mean to say anything bad. Let's just watch the ocean."

Within a few minutes Sooky began to shiver, making me cold. "Let's go home," he said.

We scurried out of our fort and headed back. I began thinking of Wake Island. It was an atoll that we only knew of as a refueling station for Pan American's China Clipper. With the Pearl Harbor attack, the atoll had become Hawaii's first line of defense. I wondered how the Marines felt on Wake Island. Were they shivering like us, waiting for the Japanese to invade?

"Major Devereux and his soldiers are brave men," I thought. As I ran toward home, I worried whether I could be like them if the Japanese came. I felt suddenly sick, remembering the war movies. A picture of a crying baby on a Nanking street flashed through my mind. I re-lived other news scenes where thousands of people ran from bombing attacks.

On this island, where could we go? What could we eat? I thought of the old Chinese proverb, "Anything that moves is edible." Would I like living on rats and birds if we fled into the hills?

With these dismal thoughts, I entered the family garage and got into my secret cache of firecrackers. The Chinese used them at New Years to frighten away evil spirits. Maybe if I made enough noise at the beach it would keep Japanese soldiers away. Besides, I really wanted to see how strong our fort was.

Heading back to the shore, Sooky caught up with me. "What you doing?"

"I'm going to blow up the fort like we blow up our toy soldiers."

"I got some paper ones, let's explode them too."

"Great idea. Get them. I'll wait by the sea."

Sooky scooted away and within minutes, returned. We set the cardboard warriors in the sand, then placed fire crackers in a row along the fort wall facing the sea. Imitating the sounds of charging men, we moved the soldiers into the attack, their faces yellowed by a crayon.

"Start firing the artillery," I ordered.

Sooky and I lit matches, the ocean breezes blew out the flames. Finally, a fuse sputtered into life and a string of loud pops exploded through the air. It was great. Cardboard soldiers flying, exploding sand stinging our bodies, the fort walls collapsing. We were ready for any invaders.

But then someone yelled, "Who's shooting? Call the police."

Oh, I knew we were in trouble. "Come on, let's get out of here," I said.

Running low, Indian style, we made it home safely. I listened for the sound of sirens and the tramp of soldiers' boots on the macadamized beach road. But no one came to investigate the noise. I knew from the silence that the island was defenseless.

* * *

Christmas in December of 1941 was miserable. A huge tropical storm drenched the island. The blackout, curfew laws, the events on Ni'ihau put fear into my heart. Worse, rationing had been imposed and food stuff on Kaua'i seized for shipment to Oahu to feed the military and the defense workers. We were unimportant to the war effort. Adding to the misery was the surrender of Wake Island two days before. Rumors spread that Kaua'i was next. Debris from sunken ships floating onto Kapa'a beaches added to our insecurity.

I didn't think we would starve, but I noticed there was no longer an abundance to eat. My dad found something good to say about our plight. "Kaua'i will never run out of fresh water." He was right, we lived next to the wettest spot on earth.

There were no Christmas trees or festive lights displayed anywhere on the island. Total blackout was necessary to prevent the enemy finding us. None of us sang Christmas carols for there was no joy in the world. Germany was victorious. Japan had the Philippines in its grasp and rampaged across the Pacific. The hope that Devereux and his marines would repel the invaders had been dashed. I prayed for the defenders of Wake Island, that they be spared beheading by the samurai sword.

Would the coming of a New Year be better? It had to be. Nothing could be worse than the uncertainty created by being defenseless. Despite the blackout, Kaua'i came under attack. A Japanese submarine surfaced outside of Nawiliwili and shelled the harbor. Suddenly, what had been movie make-believe was real. The ravages of war depicted in newsreels became part of our daily bread, for enemy submarines bombarded the outer islands and the American military was powerless to stop them.

I knew on New Year's Eve that if the Japanese invaded we could not stop them. I prayed that if an attack came my friends would remain loyal and not take the dishonorable path that the Haradas had taken.

CHAPTER 21

A Bleak Month

"Made in Japan," Sooky said as another new toy broke. There was a belief before war came that anything Japanese made was inferior to American products. This attitude of inferiority was also reflected in the restrictions on immigration and on the economic life of Japanese people in America. Before the Pearl Harbor attack, there existed a "Yellow Peril" syndrome among the establishment in the U.S. and Hawai'i.

With the destructive air strike and the rumors of sabotage and espionage swirling throughout the islands, Japanese aliens and citizens were arrested by the hundreds. By December 11, forty Japanese were imprisoned at the Wailua jail and more F.B.I. arrests were promised.

Martial law, imposed on December 7, was enforced by military courts without the right of appeal from their judgment. Everyone was fingerprinted and identity cards issued which you must carry at all times. It was claimed that spies had showed the way to Pearl Harbor by arrows cut into the cane fields and Japanese-Americans had obstructed American pilots from reaching their airplanes to fight the attackers. The U.S. provost marshal promised severe punishment for any act of disloyalty of any kind without specifying what acts were considered disloyal.

We marched off to school after New Year's. As Sooky and I hiked the three miles to our classes we talked of the war. "Japanese winning everywhere," I said.

"Yeah, the military stuff made in Japan better than ours," Sooky answered.

"The Zero fighter is faster than any other airplane in the world. It beats the Spitfire."

"I don't see any Japanese kids going to school."

"I think they're scared. People say our friends are going to prison. Japanese being picked up and have to answer lots of questions. My friend Jack says that all the Nisei soldiers in his unit had their weapons taken away, maybe they go to prison too."

"That means that nobody will defend the island."

"Jack says that there are still a few hundred local boys in the National Guard."

A silence descended between us until school. We were instructed in survival, air raid rules, first aid, what to do in a bombing attack, where to go if an invasion, and above all strict obedience to the military. There would be no boats allowed at sea, lights out at 6:00 p.m., and curfew after 8:00 p.m.

In the days ahead, military personnel came to fingerprint us, issued gas masks, and taught us how to use them in case of a gas attack. This was grim. You were told to hold your breath, ushered into a sealed room, ordered to smell the gas before putting your mask on. I remember my eyes and chest burning from the acrid-smelling, tear- producing vapors that permeated the room as I fumbled with the straps of the gas mask. I gave a huge sigh when I finally got it right.

One element of good news, the army removed its restrictions on the operation of "places of amusement." After being closed for three weeks, the Roxy re-opened. Our movies were re-runs of shows already presented, but people wanted entertainment to distract them from the gloom of our predicament. It would be months before the military allowed film to be shipped from California.

Everybody had to work. After school, my dad took me to our farm in Waialua. I was the water boy and ran to the plantation ditch, filled two buckets of water, and ran back to feed the tomatoes, beans, and carrots. It was difficult work, but my dad would point to the Japanese boy in the farm next to us yoked to a plow and pulling its furrow through the ground. "That's a good boy, a hard working boy," he said.

Though I didn't like to hear it, my father told me of his early days at the Parker Ranch. It was endless hours of labor with my grandfather being unrelenting in his criticism if Dad was "lazy." Punishment would follow if Dad continued to be a sluggard. In the old days, the credo for parents was, "spare the rod and spoil the child." I was never given a chance to be spoiled. I sometimes think that bronchial asthma came on to protect me from the strap and the stick. After all, it isn't fun beating a sick dog.

Air raid shelters were ordered and it was our responsibility to build it. We learned that the initial tactics of the enemy was to bomb the area to be invaded. As I helped dig the hole, I replayed in my mind the movies of howling Stukas dive-bombing ground targets, London on fire, and Japanese air attacks on Chinese cities. If bombers came would this shelter save us or would it crash onto our heads, burying us alive in a deep tomb? It did not help that the walls of the shelter were compacted sand. Even a near miss could collapse it.

We covered the top of the artificial cave with boards and metal roofing, then mounded sand on top. Boxes of canned goods plus gallons of water were stored inside. Then we waited for the newly installed sirens to sound the alarm.

On the test day of the new system, the crisp morning air shrieked with the screaming of sirens. Although not warning of a real attack, the piercing clangor of the alarms jangled my nerves, made my heart pump fast, and produced weakness in my legs. I stumbled with my family for the shelter, ladies first, then Dad and I. It was dank, cold, and stifling in the cave. The pipe poking through the roof was not enough to ventilate the hole or eliminate the smell of dank sand. I felt like a trapped rat. I had to escape.

"Forgot my gas mask," I said, scrambling for the exit.

Mom screamed, "Stay here."

Pulled by the leg, I slid back into the hole. "Wait for the all clear. You go out, someone will arrest you and put you in jail," Dad said.

"I'm in a tomb," I thought. "Oh, how wicked this war is."

The all clear came and I received permission to go across the street and visit Ambrose. He was in his yard with a stick gun saying, "Pow! Pow!"

"You shooting Japanese?" I asked.

"Yeah, if they come they're dead." He kept shooting at imaginary enemies.

"What do you think of the air raid shelter?"

"We haven't got any."

"Why not?"

Ambrose stopped shooting. A sad look came over his face, "Old man in jail. No shelter built."

"Why?"

"He drunk all the time."

This was tragic. There were six children in my friend's house. They had no place to run to in an air raid. "How come? All the saloons are closed. Liquor can't be sold."

Ambrose shrugged, "He knows how to find it. He got friends."

"What about your mother?"

"Sleeping around. Grandma says I'm the oldest and I have to protect the house."

What a problem, this family fending for themselves, the responsible adults either in jail or making love with someone. I couldn't let this continue. "I'm going to talk with my mother."

Hurrying home, I explained the problem.

"That's the trouble with some Hawaiians," she said. "Make a lot of children and don't take care of them. I'll talk with your father."

My dad wasn't happy about expanding the shelter. But the multicultural people in Kapa'a had survived during hard times, sharing and working together. We would survive the war by helping each other. Our family enlarged the cave and I invited Ambrose and his family to enjoy our warren when the next air raid warning came.

* * *

In the bleak days following the New Year, the Japanese swept the allies from the western Pacific. Malaya fell, the impregnable fortress of Singapore surrendered, American forces in Bataan were overrun, on and on rang the bell of victories for the Japanese. No longer could we joke that only junk was made in Japan. It appeared that the Empire was superior in every way to Britain, the Dutch, and America.

Mounting fear by those in charge resulted in the formation of a "whites only" Territorial Guard. All Nisei soldiers in the two Hawai'i National Guard Regiments had been discharged. Conscription was promoted, but Japanese were excluded. Those who wanted to express their loyalty organized themselves into the Kiawe Corps assigned to clean up areas for military camps and build roads.

If asked, I would have told them that my Japanese friends were loyal to America but years of prejudice against Orientals had risen to a flaming conflagration of hysteria generated by the attack on Pearl Harbor and Japan's victories in the Pacific. In a sense, who can blame our leaders? Fear conquers reason.

It seemed crazy when a rumor circulated the island that all non-essential civilians, women and children would be evacuated to the mainland. How could they accomplish this? Japanese submarines were everywhere. If told to go, I would live in the hills or hike into Kalalau Valley and hide like the lepers did fifty years ago.

Playing war in Sooky's sand pile I asked him, "If ordered to leave for America, would you go?"

"I don't know, but I think only the rich plantation families would be sent. Not us."

I thought about that for some moments. We weren't important enough to be of concern to the Big Five or the military. That was fine with me since I did not intend to leave, but the separation between the people of our islands was clear. It had been evident through my growing- up years that there was disparate treatment between the races. In war time a dividing line had been clearly drawn.

"What about the Japanese? My friend Hogan says that his family is worried that they will be shipped out and put in prison."

Sooky didn't pay any attention to my question as he moved his soldiers in the sand, attacking my position on the higher ground.

"Bang, bang you're dead," I said.

"No I'm not. I blew you up with my artillery," Sooky answered, pointing to a gun behind his soldiers.

I didn't think that was fair since he hadn't said in advance that he was firing his cannon before he attacked and I told him so, then added, "What about the Japanese being sent away?"

"Bobby, I don't want to talk about it," and he finished his charge up the hill destroying my defending soldiers.

Scary thoughts rushed through my mind, for the subject of ripping people from their homes was painful to consider. But this "sneak attack" on Pearl Harbor had turned everything you knew and trusted upside down. Were people you grew up with enemies? Are the helpers who weaned you from the tit and cared for you not to be trusted? What happened on Ni'ihau could reoccur on Kaua'i. Traitors assisted the Germans in their conquest of Europe. Once in power these turncoats ruled their countrymen with harshness, using the threat of death to force obedience. Hadn't Japanese from Kapa'a and a pilot ruled Ni'ihau for several days, threatening to shoot people if they were not obeyed?

I pulled away from my worries over disloyalty and focused on the current battle. "What would you do if the Japanese invaded?" I said, nodding my head toward the beach.

Sooky gazed at the ocean a hundred feet from us. "My parents talk about it. Maybe head for the hills and stay with Uncle Vick."

During his distraction I surreptitiously moved my surviving grenadier toward my friend's gun. "But look how close the mountains are to where we live," I said, motioning toward Wai'ale'ale. "We can't live up there." His attention drawn to the sheer rock walls looming several miles away, my hand moved my soldier within grenade range of his gun.

"We just have to pray to God," Sooky answered.

"Boom, your gunners are dead from my grenade. I take over your gun and blow up your men on the hill. I win."

"No fair. You're sneaky. You talk too much. I win."

* * *

Napoleon said, "The morale is to the physical as three is to one." What the Emperor meant is that the psychological effects of war are thrice as important as guns and soldiers. Unreasoned fear can defeat you without the presence of an invader.

First-generation Japanese who came as laborers retained their mother-country traditions and ties to the homeland. They were secretive and did not make friends easily. The second generation Nisei was easier to deal with. The Japanese boys had a tendency to gang together and the rest of us, whether Portuguese, Chinese, Hawaiians, or Filipinos, played with them.

Before the war, this separation was not of concern. It actually proved helpful when we played Cowboys and Indians. You could easily identify the good guys and bad guys. But with four out of every ten people on Kaua'i of pure Japanese ancestry, when war came, each of the other races was vastly outnumbered.

Nor was it possible to unite these disparate people into one combined force, because the plantation mentality had been one of divide and rule, which meant that they kept the races they imported living in separate ethnic camps. It was only in a free town like Kapa'a that the polyglot of people who left the sugar fields associated with each other. But as I have pointed out, even in this special town there was a separation. Would the social distance that the local Japanese created lead to disloyalty?

Pre-Pearl Harbor, newsreels and *Time* and *Life* magazines related the stories of respected men like Quisling and Petain siding with Germany against their countries. Jack's brother Benny had been with the National Guardsmen sent to Ni'ihau to capture the pilot Nishikaichi. I learned of the defections by two trusted Japanese to an aviator who claimed that "Japan will win the war." Their switch of loyalties was caused by family ties in Japan and promises of favorable treatment when America was defeated. In the past, the American government had restricted immigration for fear of the "Yellow Peril" and the plantations had suppressed Japanese unions. If we were invaded, could people who had been discriminated against resist a call to support Emperor Hirohito?

Because of this fear, martial law was imposed and personal freedoms terminated. Unions, strikes, and all meetings were banned. Wages and jobs were frozen. Censorship, blackouts, curfew rules, and rationing were imposed. Fishing and boat travel were prohibited. Japanese aliens and citizens were investigated by the F.B.I. Military courts conducted secret trials of those of questionable loyalty. Many slant-eyed men and women disappeared from the island.

We knew that disobedience would be summarily and severely punished. Already, shootings of fishermen had occurred. Fines imposed for blackout or curfew violations and jail sentences for speaking "bad about America." Fear that an uprising would occur gripped our island. The authorities believed that those they had suppressed would turn on their suppressors. The Big Five Companies knew the biblical saying, "As ye sow, so shall ye reap." In January of 1942 there was a belief that if a Japanese submarine landed soldiers, Kaua'i would surrender, and we'd have a Japanese day of reckoning.

* * *

"It's dark," I said, stumbling on the roots of a pine tree forest bordering the ocean. "Maybe this is not a good idea. If we get caught in the ocean, my father will strap me."

"I got no father," said Pete. "I'm not worried."

"Yeah, but if the police catch us we are in real trouble."

"What's a matta' you? No soldiers around, police busy with other troubles besides two kids fishing."

"Maybe so, but if they see you in the water they might shoot first and ask questions later."

Pete didn't answer for some moments, then said, "You could be right. I heard on Oahu they shot Japanese fishermen doing shore casting."

"Didn't know that, but Honolulu's more important than Kaua'i. All the *haole* soldiers are guarding that island. They're the 'shoot first' guys. Local boys in the National Guard are not trigger happy like them."

"The army must be real hard up for fighting men. My uncle told me the military took Juniors and Seniors out of high school, gave them guns, and put them on guard duty at different beaches."

"That's only on Oahu."

"I don't know about that," Pete said with a wry smile. "They may take kids like you and me."

"You could be right. Jack said they took away the rifles from the Japanese boys in the National Guard and they got discharged. Without them, there is nobody to defend the island."

"Not so. The *haoles* are asking for volunteers from the other races. Filipinos are signing up."

"That will make the plantations mad," I said, sliding down the berm of the pine forest onto the wet sand of the beach.

"We got to cover the big footprints," Pete said, brushing sand into the holes our feet made.

"I know what we can do. Let's walk backwards into the water just like the Indians did in *Last of the Mohicans*.

"That's stupid," Pete said. "We got to cover our marks in the sand."

We brushed the beach as smooth as we could. The first rays of morning had still not flitted above the horizon and we could barely see what we did. Stars gave us weak light. Cold water lapped over my feet and I shivered. I was naked except for a skimpy pair of old shorts. Pete had a small cloth wrapped around his crotch, all that his mother could afford. "Why did you want to go fishing?" I asked. "You didn't have to twist my arm, but you know it's against martial law."

Pete hopped from one foot to the other. I thought he was cold and trying to get warm, but he soon corrected me. "We have no food in the house. My mother has no work and we have no money. Even if we had some, rationing restricts what poor people can get, not those with money."

"What do you mean by that?"

"Ever heard of the black market? You can get what you want if you can pay for it."

"I thought that is against the law."

"You're not smart. The cops look the other way when they're paid off."

I shook my head, not understanding all the crookedness that happened in wartime. "Let's go fishing. You can have all I catch."

We slipped into the sea, the water cool and clear. I couldn't see more than six feet in front of me, it was so dark. I thought of sharks and prayed they were still asleep. No way would I know of their presence. But it's a good time to spearfish. The animals were tame and I soon had a nice string of manini and one good-sized goat fish. Green light flashed and hints of dawn colored the horizon. Low waves lapped over my head and I spotted the telltale signs of an octopus, disturbed sand with crab shells leading to an underwater hole. I could see a brown bulb waving in the sea bottom like a tethered balloon. I cocked my spear and struck it in the middle. Slimy legs sprouting dozens of suckers thrust from the hole. I held onto my spear, jiggling it in and out of the cave like a cow maid churning butter. Within moments purple ink filled the water and I felt my spear moving along the rock, pulling me out to sea. This was a big one. I rose up and called, "Pete, help me."

"Be quiet," Pete said, motioning toward the shore. The early sun's rays caught the face and body of a man searching the water with a pair of binoculars. "He's blinded by the morning light, but if you make noise or move, he will see us."

"That's easy for you to say, but this octopus is crawling around on the bottom and…" I felt a slimy tentacle searching my leg and then another set of suckers fastened on my foot. "This thing is climbing up my body!"

"Shut up. If we are caught it's our blood."

"What do you mean? Oh God, this thing is crawling up my leg, something's poking in my shorts, it's reaching around my…"

Pete's hand covered my mouth as I started to yell. "Drop your pants, put your hand by its tentacles and let the octopus crawl up your arm."

"Then it will crawl over my face and stick its fingers in my nose," I said as Pete dropped his hand and reached below the surface.

"Don't worry, I'll save you. But don't move around or make noise."

I got the idea of what Pete intended to do and I released my shorts and placed a hand where tentacles and suckers could latch onto my arm. The octopus eased its hold on my groin and edged up my arm. Both Pete and I kept our heads underwater as the creature crept towards my face. Its questing arms made me want to rise up and scream.

Pete bit into the bulb of the octopus's head and wrenched. The animal went limp. No longer did its fingers seek my nose. We rose to the surface.

"You paralyzed it," I said.

Pete brushed his palm over his lips and teeth. He squinted toward shore. A low wave washed over us without causing ripples. The man on the beach stood and replaced his binoculars in his case. "Duck down," Pete said.

I sucked air, submerged, and kicked for the coral bottom, grabbing onto a rock. How long we would have to stay underwater, I didn't know. Constant diving before the war had given me strength and I knew I could stay beneath the surface for many minutes, but Pete did not have my stamina. He was thin, almost tubercular, and he had developed the cardinal sin of smoking. I watched him a yard or so away, bubbles escaping from his mouth. He would soon need to surface. What did he mean by blood? Were the military courts like Dracula?

Pete released his hold on the bottom, rising slowly towards the surface. He did not kick, but let the buoyancy of the salt water lift him. I let go of my rock and came up with him. If we must be caught it would be together.

My goggled eyes scanned the shore. The watcher was gone. But could he be hiding among the trees? "Pete, do you see him?"

"Yeah, he's walking on the road."

"What did you mean by blood?" I said, shivering not from the coolness of the water, but the idea that Pete had planted in my mind of fangs plunging into my throat.

"Let's work our way in."

"Answer me. What did you mean?" I was prepared to be in the water all day, rather than risk being caught and blood sucked.

Treading water, Pete said, "You break the rules, the military court could send you to jail or make you pay money. If you have no money, they take your blood."

"Why?" I said, my voice trembling with the horror of the thought.

"Give it to someone else who needs it."

The ocean rolled in calm and peaceful. Above the horizon, a radiant sun lit the ocean, blessing us with warmth. A clear blue sky canopied over us, ending in huge banks of clouds to the west that hovered over Mount Wai'ale'ale. Plunging the length of its green flanks were white ribbons of foaming water. It was such a beautiful scene that for a moment I forgot that we were at war and danger lurked everywhere.

Forcing myself from my momentary hypnosis, I said, "Dracula needs blood to survive for eternity. Do other people need blood just like him?"

Pete shrugged, "I don't know for sure, but people sometimes need blood to stay alive."

I pouted and shook my head up and down, "Well, if my blood helps people live, I don't mind getting caught. Take my fish and octopus. Your family needs it."

This is the Hawaiian way. You shared what you had with friends or strangers. Unfortunately, this tendency to give without expectation of reward had led to Hawaiians living in poverty. My mother often scolded me for being generous. "If you give everything away, you have nothing, that's how the *haoles* got all the land from the Hawaiians."

Sage advice, but Pete's family had nothing. We at least had fowl and a farm. Though times were lean for everybody, I knew she would not object to my gift. Besides, if I returned home with my catch, my dad would know I broke the law and I'd get the strap.

CHAPTER 22

Bad News

An olive drab pouch holding my gas mask banged my side as I trudged up a red hill heading for Kapa'a School. Other kids walked with me, our bare feet flinging up clouds of red dirt. No one talked. There was no horseplay. We had been warned to behave on our way to and from school. We didn't need any warning, none of us felt like laughing, especially the Japanese kids.

Anything that you said or did could be misinterpreted as picking on your Japanese friends or being disloyal. At the moment, America had control of Hawai'i. But Japan ruled the Pacific, conquering everything in the path of its war machine. Many of us felt alone and abandoned by our country.

"Thanks for the fish," Pete said, hurrying to me as I walked into school. "Our army is on the run at Bataan. My Filipino friends are getting anxious. They want to fight the Japanese."

"I hope they don't start something with our local people."

"Many are itching for a fight. If anyone steps out of line, they get the knife."

"But if the Japanese keep winning and they come here, maybe it's smart to make nice to them."

"No talk like that. You go to jail if you cozy up to the enemy."

"They're not my enemy, they're my friends. And I'm not being disloyal if I treat them like I always have, good guys to be friends with."

"I could never make friends with Japanese," Pete said. "Maybe it's because they think Filipinos are inferior. They treat the Koreans and the Okinawa people the same way. The Chinese won't have anything to do with them because Japan invaded China. Maybe just the Hawaiians and Portuguese like them."

Pete's comments made me think. The only people I had trouble with were the *haole.* They were the big bosses who had taken over the Hawaiian kingdom. They refused to mix with the local people. This aloofness kept the majority of us separated from the leaders of the island. Although there was this ill feeling toward the ruling elite, I was loyal to America.

"If the Japanese invaded, would the Filipinos fight to save the plantations or because the Philippines are under attack?"

Pete smoothed over his hair made brilliant by pomade. "We would fight because of Bataan and the bombing of Manila, but we don't care about the plantations. They kill Filipinos, make us work hard but pay is poor, they don't help my mother. If somebody doesn't care for you, you don't care for them."

I waved goodbye and hustled into school. I wanted to find my Japanese friend George. He had been missing for some time. In my classes the best-behaved kids were Japanese. It isn't to say that the boys weren't aggressive. If I got into a fistfight it would usually be with a hard- headed Japanese kid. They had a banzai mentality which meant they charged into combat trying to tackle you to the ground. Portuguese like me were the big talkers and my Hawaiian side made me naughty, which was why I got into trouble.

There were times when I didn't know when to shut up and that would cost me. I wasn't a smart aleck. My mind just worked fast and I vocalized thoughts often without thinking about what I said.

To my regret, my mouth went into gear too fast when I finally found George. "Where have you been, in prison?" I said with a smile on my face.

George was inscrutable. He had the greatest poker face, but at that moment a look of distress spread over it. He turned and walked away.

"Wait up. I didn't mean anything. I'm sorry," I said, chasing after him. It took a little time to calm him down and make conversation. But he refused to talk and moved away. Something bad had happened to his family. I decided to find out what it was.

The Nisei kids in school did not want to say anything so I asked my Aunt Maggie, a teacher, "What's going on?"

"Bobby, all Japanese are under suspicion, even Yutaka. Secret hearings are occurring where questions are asked about loyalty. If you give wrong answers, they take you away."

"You think my friend George and his family went through a hearing?"

"I don't know."

"Are you in trouble because you're married to a Japanese?"

"We are under suspicion."

"Does that mean our whole family could be in trouble because of Yutaka?"

"I don't know, but don't say anything bad about America and if asked, say you're one hundred percent loyal to the United States."

"Why don't my friends want to talk about what's happening to them?"

"If being an American citizen means nothing and you are told you're bad without any reason for it, do you want to talk about it? Plus whatever you say can hurt you or hurt some other Japanese. You better remember someone could hear what you say, report you, and you're in trouble. Button your lips."

Were people I knew spies? I recalled stories about the German gestapo, men in dark suits and hats sneaking around, talking to informants, torturing people for information, and then taking victims to prison never to be seen again. Men in suits were walking around Kaua'i who were not Mormon missionaries.

I was loyal to the U.S.A., but would a stranger believe that? Could suspicion of anti-Americanism attach because my aunt was married to Japanese or because some of my friends were Japanese? It was a difficult time for all of us. You watched what you said, fearing that someone would turn you in for being un-American.

Japanese victories fueled the hysteria of the authorities. From my friend Jack I learned of an edict issued for Japanese to turn in guns and shortwave radios. Jailed aliens and suspected citizens were being shipped to Honolulu for internment.

Despite the distrust, discharged Nisei soldiers volunteered to be a work group. They were joined by others and formed into a battalion called the

Varsity Victory Volunteers. It was an auxiliary force of the Army Engineers that helped build military installations. Other Japanese leaders started a "Kaua'i Morale Committee." The reason was to give Japanese residents a chance to participate in the war effort, prevent dissension, and assure the authorities that the Japanese in Hawai'i are one hundred percent American.

From the perspective of the aftermath of World War II, it could be argued that the attitude of the American authorities was myopic and counter-productive. But Hawai'i in 1941 was perceived by Americans as a foreign land with the majority of its population living one level above savagery. The "Day of Infamy" placed Hawai'i in the forefront of the war in the Pacific and the resultant image of a "two faced, buck-toothed, dagger-behind-the-back Japanese" needed to be overcome.

Locals did not condemn them, we supported our Japanese friends and families, shopped at Japanese stores, traded with them, and shunned racial insults. This was not from a desire to ingratiate ourselves since America was losing the war. Not the case. It was the right thing to do. My cousin is Japanese and our extended family consisted of the many races that had come to Hawaii to work in the sugar fields. We were blended together as one cultural group. Discrimination among us would not be tolerated.

Strict rationing, curfews, blackouts, censorship, air raid and gas drills, restrictions on sea access, limited news, military tribunals, loyalty oaths, and other suppressions imposed by martial law created a giant prison camp of the island of Kaua'i. Every waking moment was regulated. You must have ration stamps for everything you needed. Without a stamp you got nothing.

We were fortunate to have a farm and pens with chickens and ducks. We traded food for supplies. It was not a black market where you paid extra money to get things that others could not acquire because of wartime restrictions. It was the way of the ancient Hawaiians where goods and services were shared and traded so all could survive. We lived as our ancestors, working with our hands to produce what was needed, searching in the forests for the herbs to treat those that were sick. Medicines were in short supply and ancient remedies resorted to. They worked.

I dwelt on olden times, wondering how people survived without modern conveniences that resulted from oil and electricity. I plied my mother and father with questions, but they did not want to talk of the past except to say, "It was hard times, you worked long hours every day."

In the grim set of their faces and the thinness of my belly, I appreciated that in the past they had gone without. That the Hawaiian practice of adoption, the *hanai* system, in which babies are given to relatives or friends, is a survival technique. Abortions are not part of the culture, but if a family had too many children, they were passed on to others who could care for them.

There were other practices of the old Hawaiians that I had not understood, but now because of wartime they became more relevant. I began to realize that the coming of the sugar plantations and the importation of laborers to work the fields had destroyed the well-organized farming system of the ancients that fed, housed, and clothed hundreds of thousands of Hawaiians.

We had come full circle and were back to the Stone Age with very little metal and fuel.

We wasted nothing and salvaged every scrap of iron. I realized how luxurious Hawai'i had become during the forty years of American rule.

Despite discrimination, I learned how much better Hawaii was for the Japanese laborer who escaped the poverty of his homeland and found a land of opportunity in the islands. This was true for the many others who came from Asia to work in the "land of the fragrant wood." All immigrants had good reason to be loyal to a country that gave them the means of gaining a better life for themselves and their children.

Unfortunately, Shintano and the Haradas demonstrated that roots in Japan were difficult to sever. Whether it was their disloyalty or American prejudice against the Japanese, word filtered down that internment of the Japanese in the United States was likely, a proposal that could not be accomplished. There were neither the means nor the willingness of our people to permit this action to occur.

Tensions rose. But despite the island being forty-two-percent Japanese, riots did not occur. We knew there was insufficient military power on Kaua'i to have accomplished this draconian act. More to the point, removal of the Japanese would end the sugar and pineapple economy created by the Big Five. These companies could not afford to have internment of a race on such a huge scale.

Thus, February, 1942, was a see-saw month. A period of twenty-eight days where the fate of the Japanese in Hawaii wavered between remaining in the islands or being shipped to the U.S. The anxiety of the local people heightened when news came that West Coast Japanese were relocated into the interior of America.

An omnivorous bookworm, I had read the stories of "The Trail of Tears," the enforced relocation of Indian tribes from the southeast United States into the south-west. Thousands of native people lost their lives, lands, and possessions. Despite promises by the government, these tribes were never sure of what would be their eventual home as greed generated by settlers moving west continually forced them out of territories they had been given by America.

With Japanese relocation from the West Coast, it appeared that we had a new "Trail of Tears." Ominous for those in Hawai'i, if Japanese-Americans with all of the rights of citizens could be stripped of their land and property and moved to barbed wire-enclosed camps, what about us, gripped in the vice of martial law? An undercurrent of tension pervaded the islands as we awaited the internment order for our Japanese people.

CHAPTER 23

The Coming Of "The Fighting 69ᵀʰ"

The order of internment was issued. But General Emmons, the military commander in Hawai'i, did not have the means to ship 157,000 Japanese to the mainland. More important, he did not have the support of the community. This was unlike the West Coast where the Japanese were overwhelmed by a huge Caucasian population who desired their land. Emmons was made aware that such a draconian act would destroy the economy of the islands, eliminating Hawai'i as a viable military base. Besides, who on the outer islands could have carried out the order? Only Oahu was occupied by white troops. The rest of Hawai'i was defended by a few National Guardsmen, all local boys.

The rumors of internment created a mound of worry. What would we do if my uncle-in-law, cousin, and aunt were removed from Kaua'i and shipped to America? It was not a subject openly discussed, for it might entail civil disobedience. But it was a matter secretly considered and created a new layer of uncertainty bedeviling our lives. I knew one thing for sure, none of us would have profited from the removal of the Japanese from the islands. We would have made sure that if taken away, when they returned they would get their land and possessions back. It was not the Hawaiian way to take. It may be the lifestyle of greedy foreigners, but our culture was one of sharing without expectation of reward. I know that there are cynics who will not believe me. That is because these are the type of people who take without giving back and have caused much trouble for the Hawaiians.

Japan bombed Honolulu with long range aircraft that did little damage. I didn't understand these pin-prick attacks unless it was meant to frighten us. They didn't need these raids to prove that they were all-conquering, for the war news was bad. Dutch East Indies, Indo-China, and the Philippines were succumbing to the Japanese military machine. The incendiary attacks on Honolulu and the U.S. West Coast coupled with the unstoppable advance of the Japanese army increased the hysteria of the American military who believed Hawai'i was next in line for conquest.

To meet the impending threat, recruitment began on Kaua'i for three battalions of volunteers. Japanese were banned from enlisting and the great-est signups came from Filipinos. To the credit of the local community, the shunned American citizens joined the Kiawe Corp or Victory Volunteers.

Until Pearl Harbor occurred, I had never understood the importance of oil because all work was done by hand, with pick, shovel, saw and hammer. There were no machines other than what one might find in the sugar mill or cannery. Labor was poorly paid and existence simple, rice or poi supple-mented by fish.

But the operation of boats, airplanes, and autos require gasoline. Japan had attacked because the U.S. embargoed oil from being sold to her. The resultant threat of oil starvation impelled the Empire to take the war path. As March of 1942 moved toward its dreary end I understood the Pearl Harbor raid. Severe gas rationing forced everyone to walk, slowing down the performance of ordinary tasks and ending recreational adventures. Without oil, everyday life becomes difficult and tedious.

We tightened our belts, for fishermen were banned from the sea and all civilian goods shipped in routed to Honolulu. Why? Because Oahu pro-duced only fifteen percent of what it consumed. The military needed to import food to make that island a strong defense base.

This meant that on Kaua'i we fended for ourselves. We produced or starved. This meant that clandestine forays into the sea were necessary to stay alive. On the north shore of the island were few military, and the soldiers there all National Guardsmen. They either looked the other way or joined in the fishing. For the kids in Kapa'a, we speared fish and hid beneath the waves.

Although rice was grown on the island, a problem developed. Shotgun blasts used to drive off the birds were prohibited and Japanese farmers worked overtime to scare them away. Taro was grown in fertile valleys like Hanalei, but machinery had been used for many years to grind the root into poi and trucks were used to ship the finished product to market.

With rationing, gasoline was not available. Our family reverted to the ancient ways of preparing poi, boiling the root, husking the outside by hand, and then mashing the purple bulb into paste with a stone pounder.

My dad's theater turned out to be an essential business. Movies helped morale. We got a slightly increased allotment of gasoline for our show business, but other than hauling of film or farm products, we walked. I had a bike given to me by a kindly Filipino man. My dad wouldn't buy one. He didn't believe in such frivolous things. I hid it from him lest he take it away. With rationing, it proved useful for running errands and getting to work. I had roller skates, but the roadways were too rough and dangerous for their use.

The films we showed were re-runs, mostly cowboy or Charlie Chan flicks with a few World War I shows sprinkled in, like *All Quiet on the Western Front* and *Wings*. My all time favorite war movie is *The Fighting '69th* depicting the bravery of men of that New York Irish regiment during World War I. It starred Pat O'Brien, who played Father Duffy, and James Cagney.

How did the unit get its name? During the battle of Malvern Hill, Stonewall Jackson and Robert E. Lee were standing on the high ground watching an infantry attack against the Confederate lines. Jackson says, "Here come those damn Irish again." Lee's answer, "That's the 'Fighting 69th.'"

Since curfew and blackout laws were in effect, we shut down the movies by dusk and scurried home as night came. Blackout curtains were hung in our kitchen, two bedrooms, an office, and bathroom. To save fuel, we showered in cold water, ate a cold meal, and studied lying on the floor with a lamp overhead. On rare occasions a pounding on the door created panic in the house. It would be an air raid warden who spotted a sliver of light peeping beneath a blackout curtain. At the outset of the war, wardens were lenient, but as the allies kept losing and the threat of invasion loomed there were fines and even jail for violators of the lights out policy. We soon learned that there could be a more draconian punishment for breaking the rules, death.

Waking at sunup in late March, I hurried to All Saints Gym two blocks away. Something big was happening there, for during the night trucks had rumbled along the roadway heading into the churchyard. With the sun radiating its warmth upon my shoulders, I passed by the home of a Japanese friend. He lived without his father, who had not become naturalized. I wasn't sure if he had been imprisoned. All I knew for certain was that my buddy felt unclean as if the war had turned him into a slimy creature.

Spring had arrived with a freshness that cleansed the air and the sun shone in an azure sky. Not a day to mope and worry. The mighty Wai'ale'ale lay with a mist flowing along its long green flank, ending in a halo of white clouds covering its top like a smoke ring from a giant's cigar.

Bare-footed, in my khaki shorts and light t-shirt, I raced across the government road eager for the adventure that might lie beyond the shrubs bordering the grounds of the gym. Like Carl Denham in my favorite monster movie, *King Kong*, I parted the leaves to see into the yard beyond. Holy sweet Jesus, what a sight! Dark-skinned natives were not putting flowers into the hair of the bride of Kong, but on the green lawn were more white guys than I had ever seen in my life.

I raced around the gate and scurried onto the grounds, my curiosity overcoming shyness. There were dozens of men exercising, talking, or sitting on dark green blankets laid onto the grass. A couple of men in khaki saw me coming. I thought for a moment they would drive me away and I stopped my run, staring at the soldiers.

One of the guys gave a smile and waved me closer. I shuffled forward with hands deep in my pockets. "Hey kid, you live around here?" the G.I. said.

Nodding, I pointed toward the sea then asked, "Who are you? Where are you from?"

"Name is Andy, and where, from New York."

"Have you been to the Roxy Theater? We have a Roxy here too. My dad built it after he came back from New York. "

"Hey kid, what do you call this place, Hawayah...ah...ah?"

"This is Kapa'a, Kaua'i, Hawai'i. We call it the Garden Island. It rains a lot." Several others joined our conversation. My new friend asked, "Know any girls?"

"Yeah a few, but they're young."

"Young, old, I don't care so long as they're pretty."

"Who would want to go out with a dogface like you," said a soldier.

Ignoring the remark Andy said, "What about it, kid? Where do I find these girls?"

This was getting too deep for me. I began to fidget, shifting from one foot to another. I was embarrassed by the conversation and unsure what further to say. I wanted to make friends with these men, but couldn't be a troublemaker for women like my sister. Little did I know that young girls were eager to meet American soldiers.

Andy saved me when he said, "Kid, some of us could use donuts, coca cola, hot dogs, cigarettes. Can you scrounge up some of that for us?"

Relieved by his suggestions, I nodded, saying, "I'll get you what you want, but I have no money."

"We'll advance you the dough, but don't run out on us or we'll come looking for you," Andy said with a twinkle in his eyes.

I took orders, got money, and trotted into town. Within fifteen minutes I was back and passing out packages. Some other G.I's came to me and
gave me their food orders. Off I went and returned with their meals. This
continued for part of the morning until the men had to fall into formation.
By that time I had learned that they were a company of the "Fighting 69th."
Excited by this news, I asked, "Where is Pat O'Brien?"

"Scoot, kid," Andy said, his face wreathed in a broad smile. "We have to
go to work. Don't pay any attention to what you see in the movies."

I left the yard as the men fell into formation. I watched from the safety
of the hedge as the soldiers did close-order drills. I wondered what would
happen to our island with all these blonde, blue-eyed men, hungry for girls.

* * *

In the days that followed it became crystal clear that the 69th Regiment
came to repel a Japanese invasion. Barbed wire fencing was strung along
the beaches, pill boxes poured, machine gun emplacements sand-bagged,
and revetments constructed. Daily patrols marched along the shoreline
keeping fishermen from the sea. Curfew was strictly enforced and so were
the blackout rules.

If you've seen James Cagney in *Public Enemy*, you will recognize the
rat-a-tat-tat of a Tommy gun. There was more than one night when I heard
the staccato sound of a sub-machine gun enforcing the blackout law and
someone yelling, "Turn out that damn light."

With thousands of soldiers on the island, the Japanese population
became invisible. For them it was a time of increased tensions worsened by
the military's philosophy of "shoot first and ask questions later." We lived
on an island fenced with barbed wire and guarded by soldiers angered by
having to be at war because of Japanese aggression. We were trapped in a
giant concentration camp. It did not help that there were rumors that the
government wanted to take all the Japanese in Hawai'i and imprison them
on one island. Was it to be Kaua'i?

I did okay. The soldiers needed someone to be their scrounger. I did not fail them. Soon my pockets jingled with coins as the men were generous tippers. My mother made certain I didn't keep any of my tips, but I always squirreled away a few coins from her assiduous search of my pants. Although the 69th had started as an all-Irish regiment during the American Civil War, by the time of World War II other races had been accepted, Italians, Jews, Spaniards. With this mix I learned a new vocabulary like, "Mick, Wop, and Dago."

Andy admonished me not to use those terms saying, "Those are fighting words." I hardly knew what he meant, but I heeded his advice. Besides I didn't use bad words. If I did it was confession time and endless Hail Marys and Our Fathers.

Sometimes I was asked to do a special assignment, like bring cigarettes to a beach post at night. That was dangerous. Curfew violations were dealt with severely by the trigger-happy guards that patrolled the town. Their credo, "Anything that moves at night is an enemy."

Two weeks after I had started as the chief scrounger of the 69th a red headed Irishman, who looked like the actor Van Johnson, said, "Kid we could really use some cigarettes tonight at our post by the break in the reef. You know where it is, right?"

I nodded.

"Here's fifty cents bring us a couple of packs."

I gulped, for he did not know what he was asking. I needed to sneak out of the house in the dark and hustle along the beach eluding guards on patrol using a new password every night. Plus, even if I made it to the redhead's machine gun nest, the duty officer might be there. We would all be in trouble, for smoking on duty was prohibited. Oh well, I had a reputation to uphold.

Acquiring the cigarettes was the easy part. There were no prohibitions against minors buying Camels or Lucky Strikes. But my father did not smoke and did not believe in smoking. If caught with the goods I would lose them and be severely punished. I don't like being deceptive, but I was a businessman and my stock in trade was doing the impossible.

I stashed the weeds in a hiding place at home that I knew was safe, the wood pile near the chicken house. Dinner was early that evening and my sister and I did the mandatory homework lying on the floor with a lamp between us. I became anxious, for the moon would rise somewhere around ten o'clock and shed enough light to make someone visible.

By 8:30 it was lights out and my parents retreated into the living room, my sister into her bedroom at the front of the house and I to my bed in the back. I waited for noise to end. Breathing slowly, I tip-toed out of bed, donning dark shorts and shirt to become invisible in the night. Carefully, I opened the back screen door. A hinge squeaked. Freeze. Listen. Nothing happened. With gentle movement I pushed the door wide, squeezed through, and let the door close, sighing when it did not make noise.

Scampering to the wood pile, I heard the hens in the roost clucking. I prayed the rooster guarding his flock would not crow an alarm. He had done that when rat raiders broke through the fencing that protected the roost. I froze, waiting for the fowls to settle down and return to sleep. Minutes dragged by, an eternity passed until all became quiet.

Above me the sky was free of clouds. Stars twinkled like millions of sparklers sputtering at New Year. Sound carried in the stillness of the night, and I sipped my breath to reduce the noise of breathing. I knew my path. Move low along the fence between the Japanese gardener's house and the Filipinos renting my mom's beach home. Then cross over the road, into the pine forest, and down the slope onto the barbed wire-covered beach. Problems lay ahead, the family's dog and the patrols guarding the shore. I still remembered the Tommy gun fire that recently shattered the night.

I recalled my shop teacher's favorite sayings, "Nothing ventured, nothing gained," and "in for a dime in for a dollar." I had ten cents left after my purchases. Should I risk it by trying for more? But if I turned back, the red head would no longer be my friend. He was a real nice guy. I felt sorry for these men, far away from home, without any family or comforts. I screwed up my courage and went to ground, pushing my way forward with my hands and feet. When I was even with the front bedroom of the Filipino house I heard a growl.

"Don't move," I said to myself. Frozen like a statue, I held my breath, put my hand against my thumping heart, and prayed. Someone in the house gave a command and the dog quieted. I knew that the occupants wouldn't look outside for fear of being shot.

Gathering myself, I squirmed across the grass to the county road. With my body pressed to the sand, I lifted my head, gauging the sounds of the night, seeking to detect the tramp of boots on the black-topped pavement.

Darkness lay around me, the pine tree forest that I must cross to get to the beach sighed in the evening breeze. It was a forbidding place at night, for we had dug up human bones and even found an intact skull. My mother told me that ancient Hawaiians came to this spot to die when afflicted by the *mai*, the diseases of the foreigners.

I shivered in the cool air and the thoughts of ghosts whirled through my head. Malicious talk had spread the word that the night marchers wandered this area seeking the way to eternity. My mother believed in the *kahuna* and had warned me never to travel this road at night for these disembodied spirits might seize me on their journey to perdition. Though my heart pounded, I dismissed these dire warnings, for I knew there were soldiers patrolling the beach who would drive the spooks away.

Rising, I scurried across the macadam path, reaching the first stand of trees. It was then that I recalled a rumor that the Army Engineers, when they strung the barbed wire, had also planted land mines along the shore.

It took me a few moments to consider this before I dismissed it as a false tale since we had recently played Cowboys and Indians in the forest. But the real hazard in the woods was the roots lying above the ground. They were hard to see in the dimness. The danger of tripping slowed me. Through the leaves of the forest I heard the sounds of the ocean, but could not see the water. Not good.

I came to sloping sand and slid onto the beach. Waves caused by a rising tide crashed onto the up-thrust wall of stone that formed the lagoon. Water rolled over my feet. I could not get on my belly to squirm Indian fashion along the beach. Reaching, I felt the prick of iron on my hand.

Barbed wire, nicknamed the "thorny fence," had its genesis in the American West where horses, cattle, bison wandered freely across the range. Farmers and ranchers bordered their land with fences of metal thorns taming the wandering livestock and allowing for cultivation and organized settlement of the vast acreage of prairie land. The Engineers of World War I found the thorny fence to be an excellent barrier to charging infantry. The wire slowed men down and machine guns mowed them down.

In World War II, the thorny fence was used to confine prisoners in concentration camps. I had seen their use at the Wailua jail preventing the interned Japanese from escaping. Although the military claimed it was necessary to use the iron thorns to defend the beaches of Kaua'i, I believed the barrier was meant to imprison us and prevent access to the sea.

I kept close to the slope of sand bordering the forest, seeking a path that avoided the barbed fencing. A couple of hundred yards ahead of me lay the sandbagged machine gun nest that was my destination. I judged that any patrols on the roadway would not hear my passage, for the ocean drowned out the sound of my feet. But although the sea sounds were a blessing there was danger. A wave could sweep in and pull me into the wire, trapping me in the iron mesh like Brer Rabbit in the briar patch.

The apron of sand widened as I hurried toward my goal. I left the water. Silhouetted in the dim light was the flat pyramid of the machine gun nest. It was time to be wary, for the soldiers within might not recognize friend from foe and shoot. They were trigger happy. Their uneasiness was understandable. Military necessity flung them onto a foreign land where seven out of ten people look Asian and they could not tell who might be an enemy.

Hugging the sand, I slithered toward the gun post, watching the road for patrols. The woods were thin at this point and movement on the beach could be detected from the higher ground. I wondered why the military placed the .30 caliber machine gun at this point. Yes, it covered a twenty-foot break in the rock wall of the lagoon, but a shallow coral reef stretched for hundreds of yards out to sea. Any attack boats would smash into the underwater stones and sink.

Crashing waves muffled my movements. I snaked toward the sandbags. I heard chatter from inside the dugout hole as men complained about doing duty in this god-forsaken place. For them, it was not a tropical paradise. War uprooted them from easy duty on the mainland and thrust them onto our island.

Instead of alleviating fear from invasion, they were the enforcers of martial law, the guardians of a prison. Any Japanese-American who made a misstep was punished. Already a Nisei from Kaua'i had been arrested for advocating strikes and slowdowns. We lived in an atmosphere of fear and hatred created by the "sneak attack" that made America aware of Pearl Harbor and its lagoons that housed the U.S. Pacific fleet.

"Hey, Andy. It's me, Bobby, with the stuff."

"Get in here quick," a gruff voice answered.

I slithered into the outpost eyeing the big thirty caliber machine gun set on a tripod, its snout thrusting through an embrasure in the fortification. "Have you got the cigs?" the redhead said.

"A pack of Luckys and one of Camels that I walked a dangerous mile to bring you," I smiled.

The four soldiers who manned the position chuckled, remembering the jingle that sold the paper-wrapped weed to millions of consumers. "Matches?" said one of them as he tore open the envelope encapsulating twenty smokes and shoving one of them between his lips. The others did the same and lit up from the box of fire sticks I handed them.

Brass shell casings from the bullet belt fed into the Browning glittered in the sudden light. I had never been so close to so many brass shells in my life and I felt the power of this mighty weapon that had decimated charging soldiers in the movie *All Quiet on the Western Front*.

As I admired the gun, one of the G.I.'s quipped, "This can cut you in half." His remark made me shudder, for in my mind I saw a pair of hands gripping barbed wire. I thought of the writer, Eric Marie Remarque, and the horror story that he wrote. I looked at these young boys, with their cigarettes glowing in the darkness of their gun hole. I knew that they would be the first to go into battle in the Pacific, the first to counter attack, the first to die as they brought the war to the doorsteps of Japan.

Smoking on duty was prohibited, but I couldn't blame them for wanting something like a cigarette to soothe their nerves. They were not sleeping at home in comfortable beds, but instead had to make do on canvas cots, hard floors, or beach sand. As I watched their faces become ruddy in the faint glow of the cigarettes, I said a prayer that my new friends would survive the war and come home safely.

"Beat it, kid," Andy said. "The lieutenant will be checking up soon and you better not be here." He smiled and handed over a fifty cent piece. I slithered out of the hole and headed home. My return trip, though having anxious moments, was uneventful. Slipping between the sheets I pondered over my adventure, realizing that in a police state you had to be sneaky and break the rules like curfew and no smoking, fun to do for a worthy cause like soldiers' morale. People need freedom to live their lives. Too often government makes rules that demoralize its citizens. This is especially true in a war zone where military law was imposed.

* * *

None of the soldiers manning pill boxes, machine gun positions, and occupying slit trenches along the Kapa'a beach realized that there was a Japanese fighting force inland from their positions. Mimicking the machine gun nest we saw constructed to fight invaders, a host of neighborhood kids dug a bunker adjacent to a jungle at the edge of the residences at Waipouli. We took great care to make it look war-like: rolling coconut logs to reinforce its edges and placing palm branches over its top to imitate the covering over the concrete roof of the American artillery pillbox that lay fifty yards away. This was the command post.

A few feet from our bunker stood trees, shrubs, briar patches of thorns, and tall reeds that stretched a half a mile along the shore ending at a large coconut grove. The object of the action was for one force to defend the bunker while an opposing force snuck through the jungle and launched a grenade attack using small coconuts as missiles. One hit on the palm roof was enough to blow up the bunker and win the battle. We could no longer fight with our BB guns. This was prohibited by martial law. We fashioned sticks to look like rifles and cut inner tubes into bands, then stretched one of them from the muzzle of the fake gun to a trigger mechanism near its butt.

You could not defend the fortress by hiding inside it. You had to find defensive positions in the jungle and shoot the attackers before they could hurl their coconut grenades. Of course one group of kids had to be the Americans and another group the Japanese. Who best to be the Americans but the Portuguese and Hawaiian boys and the imitators of the Japanese the Nisei boys. Those guys proved to be the greatest infiltrators. I got spanked in the butt more than once by a rubber band. Sad to say for the United States, American-Hawaiian boys kept losing the bunker to the grenades of the American-Japanese. From my experience it was easy to understand why the 442nd regimental combat team, composed of Nisei from Hawai'i was the most decorated unit in American military history with 18,000 awards for heroism.

* * *

Entertainment for the troops was deemed vital by the military. They gave priority to Hollywood movies transported to the islands. Although the bank began foreclosure of the Roxy, all civil actions were suspended during the period of martial law. Dad had taken a gamble by building a big theater, guessing that war would come and bring soldiers to fill it. Before Pearl Harbor the locals had dubbed the Roxy as "Fernandez's Folly" but now, with upwards of fifteen thousand G.I.'s on the island, our show house became the focal point of entertainment on the east shore of Kaua'i.

There were other places of amusement in Kapa'a besides our theater. Several saloons served alcohol up to curfew, a U.S.O. was under construction, and there existed a habitation where you could purchase feminine charm. Despite the threat of invasion, men of the 69th were given leave to go into town and soon these entertainment areas were filled to capacity.

My go-fer business declined as the soldiers left their camp and walked into town. I still had some scrounging orders to fill and I would head into Kapa'a to take care of the requests. What I noticed were drunken men staggering on the sidewalks heading from bar to bar. I found one poor soldier lying in his vomit in my aunt's front lawn. With her help I brought him into the house, cleaned him and put the boy to bed. My aunt washed his soiled uniform, ironing it when it got dry. Poor kid, he was only eighteen and found himself in a strange place, far away from home. It did not help that he knew he was being trained for combat and someday would be ordered to kill a human being. Something that religious training preached "is wrong."

I'm not saying these men weren't brave. But please appreciate that in those early days of America's involvement in World War II it appeared that the enemy was better prepared for war both psychologically and technologically. German soldiers blitzed through Europe. The Japanese conquered Southeast Asia. Their navy seemed unstoppable for Admiral Yamamoto knew the importance of naval air power. It appeared that nothing could prevent Japan from rolling across the Pacific and attacking Hawai'i.

With the news of daily defeats pouring in, military tension heightened. The authorities came down hard on anyone saying or doing anything considered disloyal. The results of such wrongdoing could be forever damaging. An indiscreet person was summarily tried and jailed for seditious talk. If released, he or she faced the disapproval of former friends and neighbors.

The squeeze of rationing forced the economy underground. Barter and trade replaced dollars and cents. But no one starved. If you came to a Hawaiian home you were always invited in to eat. This joy of consuming resulted in a standing joke among us, "Until she breaks the scales she is not a beauty." Hawaiian women grew up huge.

* * *

"Corregidor" is Spanish for correct. After America acquired the Philippines from Spain, the United States Corp of Engineers turned the prison into a mighty fortress. It became General Douglas McArthur's headquarters after the Japanese invaded the Philippines. Many of us believed the fortifications were impregnable and that from Corregidor would spring the counter-attack that would defeat Japan. When McArthur fled for Australia in March, gloom descended upon us. But our morale rose as the brave defenders of the island of correction resisted all efforts of the Japanese to subdue them.

McArthur issued a ringing pronouncement from Australia, "I shall return." When General Doolittle bombed Tokyo our morale rose higher. But our hopes for eventual victory were pinned on the survival of the tiny garrison on that small island defending Manila Bay.

The days dragged on into May and still Corregidor held out, fighting against overwhelming odds while the bastion was bombarded day and night. May 6th 1942, saw the crashing of our dreams when the island surrendered to the forces of General Homma. He demanded unconditional surrender or all on the island would be killed. In this darkest moment of America's fortunes in the Pacific, one glimmer of hope shone as news filtered through the censorship that the Japanese had been turned back at the battle of the Coral Sea. This unique naval battle, where opposing ships never sighted each other, halted a southward thrust by Japan to take Australia out of the war. Maybe the next move would be to seize America's last remaining bastion in the Pacific, Hawai'i?

May became a month of increased military activity. Soldiers were on alert along the coastline. We were told to stock our shelter with several days' food and water. Air raid and gas attack drills were conducted with the incessant sound of sirens shattering the nerves. There was a possibility that we would be moved into the interior of the island. Evacuation plans were issued, but, in truth, there was nowhere to go where you could survive.

Toward the end of the month, the beach defenses were manned twenty-four hours a day. Sighting drills were conducted and I watched Andy and his machine gun crew firing into the ocean, gauging distances and the elevation needed for the gun to be effective. That was how I learned that every fifth round was a tracer meant to show the path the bullets took to plow into a target in the sea.

At the beginning of June I woke to the loud rumble of engines. Heavy bombers flew over our island heading north. Something big was happening. Shuddering, I slipped under my covers, realizing that all this preparation meant that wickedness might be coming.

CHAPTER 24

The Revival Of The Roxy

Before December 7th 1941, our family worried that we would lose all that we owned. The bank foreclosed. Martial law saved us, staving off the evil day. For a brief period we were forced to remain closed by the military, but the need to bolster morale caused the authorities to relent and movies were shown again, but only in the daytime.

With the coming of the 69th the theater began to rock and roll as soldiers by the hundreds walked or were trucked into town to see the movies. They complained a lot, for the shows were not first-run movies. Despite this, the theater was a good meeting place. If a G.I. had a date it proved a convenient spot to treat a lady to a show, then take her for a soda or beer.

To save expenses everyone in the family worked. It proved a pleasant time, for we walked together to the theater and walked home after the last show, hurrying to beat the darkness. It seemed weird to start a movie at twelve noon and another at three o'clock, but the curfew hours had to be respected.

Rules regarding minors working were relaxed and other laws that infringed upon what the military considered to be vital to the war effort ignored. It seemed a strange dichotomy that all the laws that you had lived by were forgotten and war necessity made the new rules of conduct.

It was during this early period after Pearl Harbor that I heard the claim made many times, "My work is vital to the war effort." This was usually asserted when ration stamps were exhausted and the claimant wanted more gasoline. If the attendant refused to pump in petrol, the disgruntled patron would add, "You don't understand. If I can't drive to work we will lose the war." Since we were losing anyway, it seemed to me that he wasn't doing a good job in helping our cause.

Our island had to be self-sustaining since most food goods and supplies shipped in were designated for the military. There were a lot of soldiers on the island, judging from the attendance at the movies. It wasn't that the theater was filled in those early days after Pearl Harbor, but there were enough who came to make our efforts profitable.

Dad found that it did not pay to have a young pretty girl like my sister ushering at the theater. The desire of soldiers was to "make a date." One thing stood out to me, that huge Hawaiian beauties were queens during the war. Local Caucasian women were hidden from the G.I.s, so if I heard sighs and heavy breathing in the back row of the upper balcony, you can bet it involved a Big Bertha. I was circumspect in keeping my flashlight low and not shining it into dark areas of moans and sighs.

As the months wore on and the number of soldiers increased, their desire to make anything that had breasts became a welfare problem for island families with young girls. But it wasn't just unmarried women who were enamored with the G.I.s. There was an allure to the tales of the rich living available on the mainland. Plus soldiers could avoid the ration rules by buying at the PX and acquire otherwise unattainable gifts for women. It was not long before the familiar bulge in a female's belly appeared, suggesting either overeating or that the stork would soon be arriving.

Our movie theater became the trysting place where men and women could covertly meet and be transported from their worries into Hollywood's world of make believe. But the eagerness of the soldiers to bed and not wed the unlucky woman who surrendered her virtue without receiving a ring caused its share of tensions. It was not uncommon to hear a young man say, "You stay away from my sister."

Businesses prospered by being close to the theater. Short order restaurants did standing room only business, saloons continually sold out what alcohol they had, and the soda factory across the street bottled seven days a week.

The Japanese stores in town were shunned by the service men. They survived from trade with locals. Allied defeats heightened rumors of imminent internment. Soldiers who came to defend the island were hostile. Despite reasons to be disloyal, Issei and Nissei sought in every way they could to show they were true to America. They would soon get their opportunity to do so.

CHAPTER 25

The Battle Of Midway

"What's going on?" I asked.

"Can't talk about it, kid," Andy said as he lit up a cigarette that I had delivered.

"But the place is crawling with patrols. Something's cooking."

Andy shrugged. One of the other men in the machine gun post took a long draw on his paper-wrapped weed and said, "Something big is happening to the north. Leave has been canceled and we are on alert. That's all you need to know. Now scat."

Chagrined by the testiness of the soldiers, I scampered out of the sand-bagged pit. The moon had made its appearance, shining a silver path across the sea, aiming its reflected beam right at me. This was not good, for there was more military activity along the shoreline than I had ever seen.

I hugged the sloping bank of the forest, seeking to blend into the shadows made by the limbs of the pine trees that overshadowed the beach. I heard sand crunching ahead of me and my eyes darted for some hovel within which to hide. Fortunately I knew of a cave carved out by the waves in the bank. It was a perfect hiding place, covered by sagging pine branches. Ducking into it, I prayed no one heard my movements.

Marching toward my hideout were three soldiers. They were checking the wire and making repairs as needed. This was unusual. It meant that the predicted Japanese invasion was imminent. I watched them work, hearing words like, "Something big is happening at Midway."

They repaired the wire near my hideaway. Their movements silhouetted in the moonlight, I knew if I could see them, they could see me. Worried, I held my breath, keeping my body as still as I could, for their nearness made me shiver for fear of capture. Would these G.I.s spooked by a coming battle shoot at the slightest sound?

They paused some moments by my hiding place. Why did they stop? I didn't dare look, shrinking as deep as I could into the shallow cave. Sand dripped onto me and tree roots irritated my skin.

With relief I saw them move towards the machine gun nest, calling out the nighttime password. It changed every day and woe be the person who did not know it. On this night I knew it, but with my thin voice I could not fake the sound of an adult.

I watched them stack arms and dive into the gun pit. It must have been crowded with a machine gun, lots of ammunition, and six soldiers. I crawled from the cave and headed home, hoping that the men enjoyed the cigarettes I had brought.

Opening the screen door of the house, I met my mother. "Where you been?" she asked.

"Oh, outside, I couldn't sleep, too much noise from the airplanes and soldiers."

"Better get to bed. We might have to go to the mountains tomorrow. Big trouble coming."

"Invasion?"

She shook her head, tucked me in, and kissed my forehead. This was not a good sign. It meant that mom was very worried.

* * *

Although I did not learn all of the facts until much later in the war, it is a good idea to explain the Battle of Midway. It was the decisive engagement that saved Hawai'i and ended the string of Japanese victories in the Pacific.

General Doolittle's raid on Tokyo had pricked the Imperial pride in its invincibility. Admiral Yamamoto knew from interrogation of captured American airmen that the B-25s that had bombed the capitol had launched from an aircraft carrier six hundred miles from Japan. He decided to eliminate the United States Pacific fleet.

Yamamoto's plan was to attack Midway Island, a thousand miles northwest of Oahu. He anticipated that U.S. carriers would rush to defend it and planned a trap for them, intending to bring the full power of the Japanese fleet into the battle for Midway. After the American ships were destroyed by his battleships and aircraft carriers, an invasion of Hawai'i could follow.

As a diversion, two small carriers and transports sailed to attack Alaska. Yamamoto expected the American fleet to rush north. While they did, he intended to move the bulk of his war ships directly for Midway, an island between Hawai'i and Alaska. He planned to send his aircraft carriers in a left hook around the island and have them strike from the north. When the U.S. fleet rushed south from Alaska to fight for Midway, the Japanese carriers would withdraw into the main battle fleet. The Americans would be annihilated.

What the Japanese Admiral did not know was that we had broken the Japanese secret codes long before Pearl Harbor. Admiral Chester W. Nimitz, Naval Commander in the Pacific, knew of Yamamoto's plan. Despite this knowledge, the U.S. was at a serious disadvantage with only two serviceable aircraft carriers and a third in dry dock, damaged at the battle of the Coral Sea. By a herculean effort, the Yorktown was patched up and rushed to join the American task force hovering northeast of Midway Island.

Four Japanese carriers sent hundreds of aircraft on bombing strikes against the American installations on Midway. The enemy did not know of the nearness of U.S. ships until attacked by torpedo aircraft. All of our airplanes were shot down. By noon of the decisive day of battle, every American attack had been thwarted and the Japanese had found our fleet.

Akagi, Kaga, Soryu, and Hiryu turned east. On their flight decks, engines roared, filling the skies with the jangling sounds of firing pistons like the buzzing of angry hornets preparing to fly. An aircraft launched, when through the clouds Dauntless dive bombers struck, laying their

bombs on flight decks marked with the red oval of the rising sun and filled
with aircraft loaded with fuel and explosives.

* * *

In the first week of June 1942, most of us knew something serious was
occurring. "I think the Japanese are going to attack," I said to Ambrose. "If
they invade, where will your family go?"

"I don't know. We got no place to run to. You think they're coming?"

"All the soldiers believe they are."

"We'll fight them, you and I."

"With what? Sticks and rubber bands?"

Ambrose hung his head. We both believed that if the enemy came we
would not survive. That night and the succeeding nights of that first week
ending on June 7th was a time of extreme worry. At night the sound of
warplanes filled the skies overhead. I can still recall the sputter of engines
above my bed as I thought a damaged aircraft struggled to stay aloft and
reach Barking Sands Airport.

At mass on the first Sunday of the month, word spread that a great
battle had been fought and won by America. At the time, we did not know
how lucky the U.S. had been in its defeat of the Japanese at Midway.

With the threat of invasion ended for all time, the curfew and blackout
rules were relaxed. The tension in the military eased with the soldiers laughing and friendly again. A movement got underway to re-enlist Japanese-
American soldiers discharged from the National Guard. They would be
formed into a new unit, the 100th Infantry Battalion. We called it the one
puka, puka. The Hawaiian word means hole. The battalion would fight in
Europe and prove its valor at the battle for Salerno.

At first we could not show lights at night, but were allowed to walk
in the evening and visit the homes of neighbors. This was a special time,
for the family would stroll to the end of the beach road and visit with the
Keahi family. Sitting on mats spread on the lawn, we ate poi and dried fish

followed by a community sing. I can still recall lying back and belting out, "The stars at night are big and bright, deep in the heart of Texas."

Morale of the troops was foremost. Construction of the U.S.O. proceeded and the authorities decided it would be best to allow more normal movie hours, an afternoon matinee and an early evening show. My father made a deal to let soldiers come into the theater for a reduced price. The army rewarded him by trucking men into town to see the movies. I gave up my scrounger job and embarked on a new vocation.

* * *

"Hey Mac, want a shine? Only a dime," I said, pointing to shoddy shoes. "The lieutenant will like you if you look sharp with your boots sparkling in the sun."

The soldier nodded his agreement. I placed my white shoe box at his feet and invited the G.I. to put a foot onto the rectangular wooden shelf affixed to its top. From the compartment beneath the shoe I retrieved a brush and began to swipe across it, eliminating the dirt. I applied some spit to make it cleaner. Then retrieved dye and dressed the shoe with black ink followed by polish and the rubbing of a soft cotton cloth.

My customer leaned against a wall while I worked and I learned that new units arrived every day. All soldiers were into a new phase of training, jungle warfare coupled with beach assaults. Big problem for some of the men, they didn't swim.

"We're on this fake boat," my client says, "over by the river. I'm on the deck and my sergeant says "get your ass down that rope ladder." So I start with the rest of the boys, even though I'm loaded with a hundred pounds of equipment and my rifle is sliding between my legs. 'Sarge, I say, what if I fall in?'"

"'Then, swim damn it,' he says."

"But I don't know how."

"'You'll learn,' he says, and pointed down."

"Did you fall in?" I asked.

"No, but a couple of guys did. They sank. Fortunately the mock boat stood in shallow water and they could stand up. I did hear of a drowning at some time during the exercise."

What the soldier related was a problem. G.I.s came to Kaua'i without swimming experience. Several of the men in khaki would die because they did not understand the ocean, its currents, and wave action.

But the military was relentless. It did not have time to teach skills, nor coddle the fearful. The military answer to all complaints was, "We are at War and time is of the essence."

I finished the shine. Got a quarter and hustled across the road to try to con my next customer into polishing his shoes. Working the streets shining shoes was a learning experience in the ways of the world. Sex was explained to me in all its graphic details. But sometimes I wondered if what the boys in khaki related were true life adventures or fantasies they made up. I also learned craps. Gambling was illegal in Hawai'i, but there was always a noisy dice game by the side of the movie theater as the men waited for the trucks to return them to base.

To my chagrin I learned about hustlers and heads or tails. "Never challenge a gambler," the soldier said as he cleaned me out of nickels. "This is how you cheat," showing me how to hold the coin before he tossed it. He turned out to be a good guy, returning all that I had lost.

I also learned what the phrase, "why buy the cow when you can get the milk free" meant. Some of the men who came to Kaua'i were RA, regular army. They were adults. To them seducing a woman was a game. They had no intention of a serious relationship. A few drinks and some unattainable goods passed to the female, and a conquest was made. I also learned the term, "gang bang." That's where a passel of G.I.s got a female drunk and hit on her.

Shoe shining brought a good Catholic boy out of the age of innocence into the real world of men. But maybe I am too harsh on the soldiers. They were in training to die. How many would return from combat? None knew. How many would come back with serious injuries that would last a lifetime? None knew. There weren't enough ladies of the night to satisfy the boys serving on Kaua'i.

Oh, yes, I learned about "whores" also.

These are "the pay for play women," a G.I. said as I scrubbed his shoe. "In Honolulu if you see a long line of men stretching around the block to a house that's where the whores are."

"You pay for loving," I said. My incredulity made the soldier laugh.

"Yep, these gals specialize in the 'quickie'. You got two minutes to do the deed and get out."

"Wow. That fast. You don't have time to get hard."

"You better be stiff before you get into her room, because she will move you out if you're not finished and service the next guy. A hustling gal can take care of a hundred guys in a day."

This "quickie" approach of the callous prostitute taught me that love for a price is not love. It is merely an avenue to money without any meaning to the act of sex. That is not what I wanted in a relationship with a woman. I vowed to save myself for that special person. To show women respect and not treat them like an object to be plugged without any feeling for them.

CHAPTER 26

Rainbows Over Kapa'a

Irish legends say that if you follow the rainbow to its end you will find a pot of gold. But the pursuit of the colors quickly disappears as the slight drizzle that created the rainbow comes to an end.

During the 19th century, enterprising foreigners found gold in growing sugar cane. The land of Kapa'a was not wanted by the sugar planters. Most of the area, farmed by a few taro growers, was swampland. The yields from sugar cane were of low grade.

Being unwanted, the Chinese who came to work in the sugar fields and completed their contracts left the hard work of sugar cane harvesting and settled in the marshland of Kapa'a. They saw in its swampy soil the chance to grow rice. This they did. By the turn of the century they succeeded in becoming wealthy from the land that the plantations did not want. Thus for these Chinese men who toiled from sunup to sunset using human muscle power and not machines, the pot of gold for them was found in the swampland of Kapa'a.

Into the community founded by rice farmers, adventurers like my grandfather came, fleeing from the loss of his homeland Alsace. Land could be acquired reasonably in Kapa'a and it attracted people to settle in and build homes.

The growth of the town accelerated when Hawaiian Pineapple Company founded a cannery in 1913. The opportunity for work attracted hundreds of people and a town grew from the marshland. The cannery did not produce wealth for the common people, but it provided the means by which Kapa'a could grow. Not only pineapple workers came to the town, but also others interested in creating service businesses for the increasing population.

This sprouting community attracted my father to Kapa'a. He rented a hall and began the Rialto. He later built the Roxy Theater which many called a folly. But the war changed everything. Hungry for entertainment and the opportunity to meet local girls, soldiers descended on the movie house by the hundreds. The number would swell into the thousands as the military ended curfew and blackouts and allowed movies to be shown three times a day.

When the USO was completed, the results were dramatic. The town hopped with activity as the soldiers found refuge from the demands of training by coming to the movies and then attending the dances or other social events at the United Service Organization in Kapa'a.

My success at shining shoes resulted in a host of competition as other kids saw the opportunity to be gained through entrepreneurism. I began to learn another lesson, monopolies are great while they last, but competition destroys profits. So as the fortunes of the Roxy rose, my take for shining shoes dwindled. There was another factor that developed: the carving out of the town into territories. Each territory was controlled by a faction of shoeshine boys who were willing to rough up the competition. I had a haven at the Roxy for the land belonged to my family, but across the street at the U.S.O. or at the saloons along the government road the territory was claimed by different gangs.

One day I scooted across the highway to the "Blue Lei." The word had spread that a black unit had come to town and they were heavy tippers. I spied some of these soldiers going into the saloon with two Hawaiian beauties. Huge in girth, the women were dressed in filmy flower print clothes. Either of them could have been starting linemen for any football team.

I waited patiently for their drinking to end, for one of the soldiers had indicated a willingness to have his shoes shined. The wait was interminable and I almost gave up, when one of the women said, "Let's go." Here was my chance. I put on my best smile, saying to one of the men, "You promised to let me shine your shoes."

He brushed me aside. The Kapa'a to Lihue bus pulled to the sidewalk. One of the large beauties, her breasts nearly falling out of her dress, tried to squeeze through the bus door. But her ample girth was too great and she could not force herself through. The bus driver eyed her attempts with a deadpan expression on his face. The scene was so comical I giggled.

One of the soldiers scowled, shutting up my laughter. Slim as a rail, he entered the bus and called to his two buddies, "You push and I'll pull." Seizing an arm of the fat lady, he struggled to haul her in while the other two soldiers pushed her from behind. With a united effort the Big Bertha popped into the bus. The second large lovely turned sideways and the pulling and pushing commenced again until she finally stumbled into the vehicle.

During these efforts, the driver looked on impassively, his inscrutable expression never changing. But when they all sat on one side of the bus and the vehicle tilted, his eyebrows went high. He said nothing, closed the door, and drove off. The bus cocked at a right angle as it sped along the highway.

My waiting for business cost me. The boss of the territory around the Blue Lei threatened to wallop me if I didn't leave. I might have made an issue of it, but there were several other shoeshine boys coming to enforce his order. Retreat seemed the better part of valor and I hustled across the street to the Roxy.

* * *

When the military raised the curfew hour to 10:00 p.m. and allowed the theaters to stay open to 9:00 p.m. our movie business took off. It helped that the USO across the street started dances after the shows. The local girls did not know how to jitterbug, but many of them knew how to hula. However, the servicemen rejected that dance as too slow and not provocative enough. They had expected a strip tease with females clad in skimpy outfits that could easily be removed.

To remedy this deplorable situation the USO imported "Flying Squadrons" of girls from Honolulu to be dance partners. Some of the Kaua'i females began to learn the mainland routines and soon the most popular places on the island were the Roxy and the USO building.

In Kapa'a alcohol was consumed as fast as the brew could be distilled. The bars on the main street were open from morning to curfew time. Anyone but minors could buy drinks. That was okay with me. My father didn't drink and I couldn't stand the stuff. The importance of the half dozen saloons that opened in town was that they brought soldiers to Kapa'a. Thus, alcohol, dancing girls, and the movies made our Roxy the in place to be, especially for the late afternoon matinee.

I like to speak of Kapa'a as a place where poor people could come, acquire land, build a home, start a business and prosper. The Chinese had proven the worth of the marshland surrounding the town by clearing, cultivating, and growing rice in it. They became wealthy from selling that crop.

My father was a poor landless Hawaiian when he came to Kapa'a to operate his movies. My mother was poor. She was one of twelve children and her dad a field supervisor for the plantations.

When Pop built his grand theater, everyone laughed at him. But now the thousand-seat theater was filled to capacity day after day. His foolish pride in copying the Roxy Theater in New York paid off because of wartime. But consider the gamble if Japan had not attacked when it did: he would have lost everything. If martial law had not been declared he would have lost the theater. If soldiers had not come to defend the island and train for jungle warfare, he would have lost the theater. But his gamble paid off. Business was so good that he paid the mortgage by Christmas and had money in the bank. Two poor Hawaiians had found their pot of gold at the end of the rainbow in the mud of Kapa'a.

CHAPTER 27

Politics and Barbed Wire

"Bill, you were a Republican in the House of Representatives and understand politics as well as anyone. Should I withdraw my nomination for re-election?"

"Yutaka," my father answered, "you have been a great Chairman of the County Board of Supervisors. I know our Republican leader on Kaua'i has said that Japanese should not be in public office, but you and the other four Japanese men who are running have proven yourselves as capable politicians. You will all be elected by a landslide."

"But Bill," interrupted my Aunt Maggie, who was always outspoken in any conversation, "you haven't read the newspapers. They demand that 'subjects of the Mikado' withdraw from political office. They say, 'If Japanese in Hawai'i don't like that, they should go back to the land of their ancestors.'"

"And the *Garden Island* has just come out with an editorial," Yutaka added, "urging the withdrawal of all Japanese political candidates for the good of the Territory. The editor claims it is our 'patriotic duty' to do so."

I sat in the far corner of the parlor playing with my Japanese cousin. At the time I did not fully understand what I was hearing since children are taught "not to speak until spoken to." But during the fall months of 1942,

I pieced together the sad story that had brought us to my aunt's home. The anti-Japanese sentiment against Nisei politicians had struck the family like a thunderbolt.

Yutaka Hamamoto was an American citizen. He had a degree from the University of Hawaii and a prominent job in agricultural research for the Territory. My uncle-in-law had swept into office with three other Japanese-American citizens before war came. They broke the Republican stranglehold on the government of Kaua'i. Serving as Chairman of the Board, Yutaka was instrumental in re-planning and re-zoning the towns of Kaua'i. This the plantations did not want. They desired that land use be kept agricultural and hence their taxes would remain low.

More to the point, both Houses, Senate and Representatives, were dominated by Republicans. A trickle of Japanese had succeeded in acquiring seats. If the outer islands had Japanese supervisors in office and more Nisei candidates ran for election, the political power could shift to the Democrats. When forty percent of the population is Japanese there is no doubt that they could "upset the political applecart."

"Hamamoto, you are in a tight spot," my father said. "The war with Japan has brought back the prejudices against the Oriental that we thought buried long ago. The Republicans want all Japanese candidates to withdraw. Would this be good for Hawai'i? I don't think so. But if you are elected, the plantations will come after you. Senator Abe has been put in prison for having a Japanese flag in his house. In Koloa, a Japanese union leader has been arrested for distributing union news at lunch time. While in office, you will be under tremendous scrutiny. One wrong word or move and you are in trouble."

"And a Japanese boy is in jail for saying 'The U.S. Army is no good,'" my aunt added, her voice shaking. "Say the wrong thing and we'll be arrested and sent to the mainland."

I reached my hand to my young cousin, placing it on his shoulder as a sign of reassurance. The family would never let him be taken from his island home. But could we stop the military from seizing my Japanese relatives and putting them into a concentration camp? Martial law had eliminated our rights. There were plenty of American soldiers who would enforce orders. Clutching Joseph's arm, I prayed that he not be taken away.

"Big decision for you and the other Japanese candidates," Dad said. "Surrender to the pressure and Hawai'i stays the same, under the control of the Big Five."

"Thanks for your help," Yutaka said. "I'll talk it over with the others."

A couple of days later my uncle-in-law and the other Japanese men withdrew their nominations for election to public office. The Governor praised their decision. It was not a victory for the people. The plantations had won. The bulk of the population was still subservient to them.

* * *

"You have to help dig up the back yard," Mother said.

"Why?" I answered, chagrined that I could not run off to town and shine shoes.

"We must plant 'Victory Gardens.'"

"Why? We have a farm in Wailua."

"Don't keep asking why." I could see Mom was getting angry. Kids were not supposed to talk back to adults. But I wanted to know reasons for her order since I had a business to take care of.

"Can't you tell me?" I asked, pushing the situation to the edge of a spanking.

"We don't have enough food to eat. Everything coming in is going to Honolulu. So we have to grow what we need and send what is left to Oahu."

"But can't we live on fish?" I persisted in my inquiries, delaying the time when I had to begin working.

"Don't you see all the barbed wire blocking the beaches? Fishing boats can't go out to sea. We must grow what we need or starve."

Her conclusion awoke me to reality. We could not fish from the shore and the sampan fleet had been quarantined. These fishermen were aliens. They sailed vessels that were twenty to eighty feet long, with a sharp bow, hut in the center, and a large wide stern. Powered by diesel engines, sampans could travel a thousand miles out to sea in search of tuna. The authorities suspected the boat captains of being smugglers of opium or saboteurs.

When war came, the vessels were tied up for the duration. It was believed that the Japanese operators would spy on the U.S. fleet and notify Japan of what was happening in Hawaiian waters.

I began to dig up the grass, still complaining. "What about Makario? Can't he help?"

"He's joined the army like other Filipinos. Everybody is short-handed. Any men not drafted are heading for Honolulu to work. They make more money than on the plantations. There is lots of military construction going on behind Sleeping Giant and at Barking Sands. Plantations have lost a lot of workers. There is talk of letting twelve-year-olds work in the sugar fields."

This was interesting news, for unless you were employed by the family, child labor laws prevented businesses from hiring below the age of four-teen. I later found out that the plantations and canneries were desperate. They lost more than a third of their pre-war work force to the war effort. Interesting enough, the plantations were able to make do by mechanization. Their production of sugar during the war did not falter. It remained at peace time levels.

The pineapple canneries proved to be survivors, as well. They made it by using child labor. All school children were expected to donate several days a month to work in the fields or in the public schoolyards.

You ask, "Who bought the canned pineapples?"

The military did.

Sugar cane was still being processed and shipped to the West coast to be refined and sold. The agricultural economy did not suffer during the war. Wages and jobs were frozen. This maintained the profits of sugar people, but the big question remained, what would happen when peace came?

Despite the home victory gardens and land requisitioned from the sugar plantations by the army to grow potatoes and vegetables, there continued to be a shortage of food. Oahu consumed all that the outer islands could send and still needed more. The military viewed Honolulu as its most important outpost in the Pacific and the soldiers and workmen there must be fed. The outer islands became the supply line for Honolulu.

Our farm, lying beneath Sleeping Giant Mountain, was considered essential to the war effort. We did not have machinery or running water. It was hard work to keep it up, for everything had to be done by hand.

Water came from the nearby irrigation ditch, carried in buckets from the sluice to the growing crops. I used pick and shovel to turn the soil and form plant beds. Raking leveled the ground and the hoe created furrows and removed the rocks embedded in the earth.

Tomatoes were our primary crop and growing them was labor intensive. Pinch out the off shoots from each branch. Stake each shrub so it will grow straight up and not spread out over the ground. When the blossoms came, reduce the number of fruit by eliminating buds. When the tomato greened, wrap each one in a paper bag to prevent the sting of the fruit fly. This creature is the bane of the farmer. Its laying of eggs in the tomato will rot it and any fruit adjacent to it. The saddest moment for us came after we harvested our first crop of ripened tomatoes, packed them into boxes, and shipped them to Honolulu. The distributor called to say, "A number of boxes are rotten." The sting of the fruit fly had tainted what we had shipped.

Each day I looked out beyond the barbed fence that kept us from the sea. There were fish out there waiting to be caught. But wire and machine gun nests hemmed us in. The soldiers had all the food they needed. But we were trapped in a concentration camp and not allowed to fish or access the sea for something to eat.

CHAPTER 28

Troubles In Paradise

A laid-back, stress-free island that typified life on Kaua'i was forever changed by the attack on Pearl Harbor. Folks who had survived on hard work, kids who had never thought of health problems, multi-races that had lived in harmony, were beset by unexpected troubles created by wartime.

As an example, I arrived at school and saw a van with "TB" stenciled onto it. The school nurse at the vehicle's door said, "You must go into the van and be x-rayed."

My curious mind forced me to protest. "Why?" I said.

"TB has increased in the island. Everyone is being checked. You will be injected for smallpox, also."

I looked at the raised scar on my arm. I did not want to be stung by the big needle again. After an inoculation, you were sick for days.

"What's going on?"

"The health department is worried. Disease is rising. The black plague has been reported in Hilo. Dengue and typhoid fever is making many people sick. In you go." The nurse ordered me into the van and like a good boy, I entered and got x-rayed. What the nurse said troubled me. What did this increase of disease mean? Were the Japanese conducting germ warfare?

They had been flying long-range reconnaissance aircraft over Honolulu and dropping incendiaries - had they switched to bacteria bombs?

Wartime brought with it a Pandora's Box of ailments and rumors that proved more deadly than an invasion. Speculation existed that the lack of healthy foods, anxiety, and over- work had sapped the stamina of the island people. No one knew the answer. The specter of an epidemic hovered over Hawaii. There were people still living who remembered the Spanish flu of 1919 that killed thousands.

Because of the fear that the Japanese could use American money for spying, all currency had to be turned in. New bills were issued with "Hawaii" stamped on the face of each bill. Failing to do as ordered meant that if you were caught with an unstamped bill you would be considered a counterfeiter or spy and punished. This created a problem for older people who did not understand what to do or did not trust the government. Unstamped money kept showing up.

Servicemen returning from wartime experiences in the Pacific were hostile to waitresses, bartenders, and busboys who looked Oriental. From Honolulu came word of beatings of American citizens of Asian descent. When half of the people in town have an Asiatic look, who can tell the difference between the good guys and the enemy who had shot at you in the Solomons or Tarawa? Ads for help at retail and commercial outlets had a tag line, "Japanese need not apply."

Kaua'i did not have as huge a problem with racial animosity as in Honolulu. But the hostility of the soldiers on my island was evident. They said insulting words like "yellow belly," "slant-eyed bastard," "Buddha head."

It was clear from the mainland news that Americans were shocked at the number of Japanese living in the islands. They wanted to know all the treacherous facts that had been perpetrated at the time of Pearl Harbor and after. Some believed that this foreign Asian population would rise up in revolt and seize the islands for the Emperor of Japan.

These perceptions tainted the thinking of the men who came to Hawai'i to fight the war in the Pacific.

It was these prejudices from the mainland that forced out of office every Japanese-American legislator. The new year of 1943 arrived without a single Nisei in office.

CHAPTER 29

The Turning Of The Tide

We were winning in the Pacific. With Guadalcanal securely in our hands
and New Guinea rid of Japanese soldiers, Australia was safe. On Kaua'i
fifteen thousand men prepared for the invasion of the Philippines. A
"Gung Ho" attitude pervaded the island.

War movies like *Wake Island* and *Bataan* played to packed houses. Even
though these battles were American defeats, the words by the actors were
stirring as they performed heroic deeds against impossible odds. Roxy
crowds cheered when American soldiers wiped out hordes of attackers. It
was astounding how high morale can soar because of the propaganda effect
of the movies.

Our local Japanese were smart enough not to patronize these films. It
was not a boycott, but rather avoidance of unwanted trouble. Among my
Nisei friends there was an undercurrent of loyalty to the U.S. building
toward a high crescendo. It was not American victories that caused this
increase in patriotism, but a burning need to secure the respect of the people that hated them. The 100th Infantry Battalion, composed of Japanese
boys from the Hawaii National Guard, was in training at Camp McCoy
in Wisconsin. Hawai'i Nisei wanted a chance to join them and fight for
America.

General Emmons announced that the war department had authorized the enlistment of an all Japanese-American unit of 1,400 men. As soon as the call went out, almost ten thousand Hawai'i Nisei volunteered. The size of the unit was increased to 2,600. With American flags waving, Japanese citizens cheering, and young men smothered in garlands of flowers, the largest crowd ever assembled in Hawai'i bid these volunteers farewell when they boarded ship and headed for the U.S. They left with the prayers of all of us that they would prove themselves to be loyal Americans.

* * *

I surfaced with a large red fish wiggling on my spear. "Look Pete, I caught this big kumu."

My Filipino companion gave me a wry look as if to say, "I'm the one that should have caught it." I knew his family needed fish more than mine did and I knew how they would cook the goat fish, steam it in soy sauce, ginger, and scallions. Oh, what a meal they would have. I silently promised to give it to him.

I threaded the kumu onto a cord attached to a strip of balsa bobbing upon the surface of the ocean. I pushed the red fish to a half-dozen manini suspended under the water at the balsa end of the cord. The entire array looked like a necklace of colorful fish floating in the water.

Pete swam away, searching for quarry. The sun shone on lazy combers slowly rolling over the up-thrust stone protecting the lagoon and then spreading out onto the shore. Barbed wire stretched for miles along the coast. It had been a difficult task working our way through the iron thorns. Fortunately, we had found a weakness in the barbed defenses, paid a price in scratches and blood, before finally entering the sea. More than a year had passed since we had been denied access to the ocean. Although the sampan fleet could not sail, there was no longer a prohibition against shore fishing. At least I hoped so. The soldier boys no longer guarded the beaches. They were inland, fighting war games and conducting maneuvers.

It is difficult to describe the beauty that fills your eyes when you submerge beneath the waves. Lush forests of sea weeds and coral spines thrust from the bottom like petrified forests. Multi-hued tropical fish flit between jagged rock formations, teasing you before disappearing. Bright sun pierces the water, lighting what is under the surface with a golden glow that fades into hues of blue that grows darker and ends when you can see no farther. You are drawn toward what is hidden by invisible harpies mesmerizing you with their song of the deep, an inviting tune that draws you downward to find what exists beyond what you can see Skin diving combines the skill of the huntsman with the passion of the explorer who yearns for the excitement of discovery. The sea is frightening. Its currents are deadly, its tugs and pulls unpredictable. Your reward is what you discover as you stalk through the water.

Mainland soldiers during their time on Kaua'i drowned for failing to respect the power of the sea and understanding how to deal with its whimsical behavior. But if you have knowledge of its ways, then you can easily survive. My ancestors had journeyed thousands of miles across the waters to discover and populate Hawai'i. For them the ocean was not sinister, but a friend, for it provided food to sustain them on their long voyages of discovery.

"Kala coming," Pete yelled, waking me from my reverie. I looked toward the sound of his voice. I saw the familiar shingle-shaped fish wiggling its thorn-covered tail in a rapid fan beat, thrusting the fish toward me. A protruding eye stared either from fright or anger. It was not a fish to argue with, for it had a blunt shaft sprouting from its forehead like the horn of the unicorn.

Pulling back on my rubber sling, I let fly. My spring steel spear leaped from the bamboo tube like a torpedo fired from a submarine. The sharp pointed front of the shaft plunged into the leathery olive-green hide of the fish, halting it in its rush to flee. Wiggling to rid itself of the iron thorn in its side, the Kala hit stone and then plunged into a crevice in the reef. The end of my spear waved like a wind tossed pole as the creature fought to wrest itself from the shaft embedded in its side.

Pete came to me. "You got him."

"The skin is tough. I don't know if the barb went through. You whack him one more time."

Pete dove, searched the crevice and fired his spear. Both spears wiggled as the Kala fought our missiles. But Pete's shot proved the *coup de grace*. He pulled the fish from the hole and offered it to me.

"You take it. Your family loves to make steamed Kala. Watch the thorns at its tail. When it wiggles they can slice like a razor."

Pete gave me a grateful smile, returned my spear, threaded the fish onto his line, and swam off in search of more prey. Contented, I rolled onto my back and floated, searching the blue sky for clouds. My thoughts drifted back to an earlier, happier time before the war.

* * *

"Hold the pole straight," said the Reverend. "Let the net billow out with the current. When the Kala comes, wait for my signal then move towards Raymond, closing the trap."

"But how do we catch those big fish? The eye of your net is too small to gill them."

"They will run into the purse in the center."

"But they will turn around and come out."

"Fish only know one way, go straight. They will stay inside the pocket and we will get them."

The Reverend angled towards the shore, then moved diagonally toward a position a hundred yards away. Two other boys aligned with him, paralleling the crescent shape of the net. For two days, the lay minister had watched the school of Kala cavorting along the reef, feeding on the tufts of sea weed that spread across the bottom. He waited until this evening when light faded into dusk. With the darkening of the day, the net would not be easily seen by our prey. He expected they would bump into the mesh and follow its curve into the pocket in its center.

"Bang. Bang," came yells across the water as the Reverend and the two boys shouted and pounded their palms onto the sea. The triumvirate of ocean beaters advanced toward the net.

I searched the water for scurrying animals. I saw none. This entire venture was a failure, I thought as I stood in the surging water like a dummy, holding onto a stick. A slithering body sped past my bare leg, smashing into the net with such force that I almost dropped my pole. The minister had warned me not to do that. Saying, "Keep the stick up so the buoys at the top of the net ride on the surface."

More slimy things rushed past. I could feel them smashing the mesh, nearly pulling the pole from my hands. A great commotion occurred in the center of the net where the purse billowed in the current.

"Move towards Raymond," yelled the minister.

I did as ordered and closed the trap with the help of the other boys. We hauled in thirty- five of the tough-skinned Kala. But the best part of the adventure was the party afterward. The reverend's elder son Elmer played the guitar and Raymond the ukulele. We sang songs and even had a hula or two. It was good fun.

* * *

A wave covered me, ending my dream. I treaded water and looked toward shore. Barely visible rose the mound of the camouflaged machine gun nest. Its observation slit across the front was darkened, obscuring the instrument of death hidden in the shadows. I knew the power of the gun. Andy had shown me the weapon in action.

"Fires five hundred rounds a minute," he said. "Watch as I check range."

The Browning chattered, flinging out brass casings from its chamber. The loader fed the weapon from a belt of lustrous shells. Bullets ripped the sea flinging spurts of water into the air.

"You can follow the line of fire by the tracers," Andy said. "Every fifth round shows where we are hitting."

"What's the rubber tube and can for?"

"Water to cool the gun, this baby gets hot in no time."

I began swimming away from the dark maw of the machine gun's lair. In my mind, I visualized the bullets tearing into my body, ripping it apart. I had been told by my elders that the *kahuna ana ana* could do that. He could utter his death chant and his string of words would rip you to shreds. "Only the hiring of your own kahuna can counter the death chanter," an old Hawaiian said.

Never had I seen a sorcerer hurl words at another and destroy him. But watching the Browning in action taught me that bullets, not words, will rip you apart. The soldier boys had real power, death-dealing power that you could see. I realized that the men from New York had brought a new reality to the islands.

Thorn fencing stretched along the coast line until it vanished from view at the old slaughterhouse where blood once flooded into the sea from gutted animals. Sharks had once swarmed there to fight over the entrails of dead beasts. Today, an artillery pillbox defended the shore and machine gun nests covered the danger spots where an attack might come to destroy the cannon.

The defenses of the island were not Hollywood make-believe, but the real thing. Over the preceding year Kaua'i had changed into a fortress. Its population had increased by a full fifty percent with all the soldiers in training and workmen who came to build facilities. We were no longer an unknown dot on the world map, but on the front stage of war in the Pacific.

"Wake up. What you dreaming about?" Pete yelled.

Startled by his demand, I said, "Life has changed. It is no longer 'do it tomorrow.'"

"What?"

"Let's go in."

We swam towards shore, my fish line tangling in my kicking legs until I unfastened the pin from my shorts and grasped the line in my spear hand. With my other arm, I stroked toward shore, aiming for the break in the wire. Why tell the military of the weakness in their defenses? No one believed that the Japanese would ever invade, for the American news continued to announce a string of victories.

After we worked our way through the wire, Pete and I stood away from the beach. He admired his Kala, saying, "Make good soup." Then he gave me a hard stare. "What you mean, 'life has changed?'"

"Before the war, sugar plantations ran everything. Keep us out of the cane fields. Make us live in Kapa'a. No can go where the *haoles* live. War comes and military takes over. They tell the plantations what to do. Maybe time for us to wake up."

Pete palmed his hair, smoothing out the tufts that sprang unruly above his scalp. His eyes narrowed and his brow furrowed as he thought over this new idea. "My father came to work for the plantations to make enough money to return home and live like a king."

He paused and I said, "But he didn't make money, left sugar, and married Hawaiian."

"And we lived as if the plantations still controlled us," Pete answered.

"So maybe the soldiers have come to teach us that our life has changed?"

Pete scratched his head and shook his face from side to side. "I don't know. Maybe?"

He turned away, trudged toward the railroad track, heading for home. I watched him go, realizing that it was difficult to accept that the war had washed away the century of control that sugar had exerted over the lives of all who lived in Hawai'i.

CHAPTER 30

Work To Win

Before war came, it had been drummed into our family that labor laws prevented children from working before the age of fourteen. Exceptions were made if you helped in a family business. This law of the United States applied to the territory of Hawai'i. It was a rule that allowed my mother to have some schooling until she reached the age of fourteen and was put to work at the new pineapple cannery that opened in Kapa'a. Her family needed the four cents a day she earned to provide the means for her elder brothers to get an education in Honolulu.

My father did not have this advantage. Hawai'i was a monarchy at the time of his birth. His dad snatched him from his home at age eight and put him to work on the Parker Ranch on the "Big Island." My father regretted his lack of education. At fifteen, he ran away from his cowboy life, came to Honolulu and went to school. Five years later, Hawai'i became part of the United States and the plantations acceded to American law.

My father preached education. He wanted me to become a lawyer and be smart enough to "catch those who tried to swindle and cheat." Despite him and three relatives who lectured me on the virtues of reading, writing, and arithmetic, I had grown up apathetic to the whole idea of education. Life was simple when you had nothing. Without stress to acquire things, what you made with your hands was the real value in life. The Christian work ethic was a fine idea for those who were old. It was not for me.

Besides education, my dad preached working hard. That had been his life growing up. There had been nothing carefree about his upbringing and being a self-taught, self-made man, he was hard on his only son. I'm afraid to say that asthma let me break away from obligations. But I could not let illness make me be an invalid. Spear fishing brought me back to the land of the living with all of its responsibilities.

War had come to Hawai'i with its heartache and pathos, bringing with it new responsibilities. To save ourselves, islanders needed to conform to martial law, be self-sufficient, and in the second full year of the war, "Work to Win."

This was a most unusual demand. It did not come from the military, but from the governor. It was not a work program for the many, but designed for school children twelve years and up. The whole concept had been resisted by educators, but finally they gave in to the needs of sugar and pineapple.

I asked my Aunt Maggie, "Why do they want kids to work? Aren't there laws saying you have to be fourteen to cut and pick in the sugar and pineapple fields?"

She gave me a deadpan look, her eyes penetrating my brain. "Most of the plantation men and women are working for the military in Honolulu. Other folks on Kaua'i are working in construction. The sugar and pineapple fields are without manpower to harvest crops." My aunt sucked in her breath then continued, her usually calm voice agitated. "Over my objections, the district has given up the fight to keep you kids in school. Everybody twelve years or older must donate time to help out either at school or in the fields."

"Well, that leaves me out," I said. "I'm not twelve yet."

"You'll be twelve this year. That makes you eligible."

What a stunning revelation. Wartime meant that the usual rules no longer applied. I soon found myself working in the afternoons at the schoolyard pulling weeds and as summer drew near, the prospect of full time work in the fields loomed.

I spoke to Mom, who once worked for the Pono Cannery. She said, "I'll find a job for you picking pineapple. Your father will let you do it because it's patriotic."

My first day on the job arrived. I stumbled out of bed at 4:30 in the morning. My mother packed a lunch tin and at 5:00 a.m. I stood at the gas station by the main highway with several Japanese women and a Nisei friend that I hadn't seen for a long time. Despite my cheery greeting, he was non-committal and I ended the one-sided conversation. A big stake truck showed up with other workers on board. We piled into the bed of the vehicle.

A stake truck is nothing more than an auto with a flat bed, fencing on two sides of the bed, and chains enclosing the rear. The driver was either drunk or loony, for he drove like a maniac and took curves in the roadway at breakneck speeds. The human cattle herded together pitched to and fro from one fence to the other and from cab to chains. It was a truck ride more frightening than being on a roller coaster. At any moment, I thought, the wooden stakes plugged into the truck's bed would break and the mass of humans would tumble out onto the roadway or over a cliff into a ravine.

Bruised but not broken, I tumbled off the truck into the pineapple field. Like a Cyclops' gigantic eye, the hole in Anahola Mountain glared at me. It was claimed that after a storm had destroyed his invasion fleet, the great king Kamehameha hurled his war spear in frustration. The shaft penetrated the mountain above me, creating the eye.

Of course that is only a legend, but it is true that the eventual ruler of the islands lost thousands of men and canoes trying to invade Kaua'i. Our *kahuna* uttered death chants to keep him away. They worked.

An interesting fact about the early days of pineapple growing in Hawai'i was the anemic look of the first plants. They grew shrub high, flowered, but as the first buds turned into fruit the leaves became a sick yellow color. Death of the plants appeared imminent. Frustrated, the growers sought an answer from experts.

They were told, "The plants are iron-starved."

"But look at the soil they are growing in," the planters said. "It is orange red and rich in iron."

"They need iron sulfate," came the experts' answer.

Rusted cars, oxidized iron, or a spray of sulfate were introduced to the fields to save the dying pineapples. This story seemed unbelievable to me as I stared at the rows of sharp spiny shrubs whose roots thrust deep into ochre red soil and were crowned with large yellow fruit the size of a football.

Scores of wooden boxes were stacked along the dirt roadway that traversed the rows of growing pineapple. A woman *luna*, field boss, yelled, "Grab boxes, put them by the rows I assign you. Fill each box with pineapple. Remember to save the crowns."

She gave me ten rows to harvest, each row the length of one and a half football fields.

I took a deep breath and ran as fast as I could to the end of my first assigned row. From watching other pickers I knew I had to work fast, I knew I was not paid by the hour, but by the boxes that I filled. A loaded box had sixteen to eighteen pineapples in it.

I didn't know how to pick the fruit, but watching others, I learned to seize the body of the pineapple, twist, and dump the three or four pound grenade-shaped fruit into a pitas bag, a hemp sack with ropes for handles. A big problem for me was my hand did not fit snugly around the thorny fruit. I needed to wrench, pull, and leverage the pineapple from its perch.

Pineapple is not a beautiful fruit. The shrub it grows on sprouts like a briar patch of sharp green spears. The body of the fruit has a thick green-yellow hide layered with thorns. Nature made sure that anyone disturbing a pineapple will be stabbed. Despite my heavy gloves the sharp spines poked and slashed my wrists.

Too soon, the sack was unbearably heavy and I staggered to the start of the row to dump my burden, then ran back and kept picking. Once I cleared my row, the removal of the crowns began. Twisting them off was an option, but clusters of spiky leaves easily pierced my gloved hands as I squeezed. The best answer was the karate chop. Using my extended palm like an axe, I hit and hit until my boxes were packed.

There was no time to rest. More rows must be harvested. Off to the next row and the next, repeating the drudgery. The sun rose blazing hot. Throughout the day, sweat drenched me, for I was covered with tough cloth from my hat to my boots to protect me from thorns. Pineapple juice soaked my clothes. The sun baked the drenched garments into a warm, sweet, sticky concoction of pineapple sweat. By the time I finished the day, I smelled like rotten fruit, my slashed hands hurt, and my blistered feet ached.

Arriving home, Mother greeted me with a broad smile and happy chatter. She helped me undress and remove my boots. "How was your first day?"

"Hard, stinky, and hot," I answered. "When I grow up, I want an inside job so I won't smell like Johnny pineapple."

Mom laughed, saying, "I worked for years inside the cannery. It was hard work, but not hot like in the fields. Maybe you learned something today."

She was right. I think it is from that moment I decided to become a lawyer. Better to suffer in a cool courtroom where the only heat is words. I did make a big mistake by telling her about the reckless driver and our wild ride. "He was just like Toad in *The Wind in the Willows*."

Before dawn the next day, I shivered with the others for the dreaded ride in the stake truck. Amazingly, it was a pleasant experience. The driver did not speed. He took the curves in the roadway at a reasonable pace without causing the work crew to bounce from one stake fence to the other. When we got to our assigned fields, the driver did something startling. He got out of the truck holding a long bolo knife. With his eyes blazing and his face livid with anger, the driver pounded his weapon on a crate,

flinging slivers of wood in the air. Glaring at the frightened group huddled
near the boxes, he growled, "Who is this Bobby Fernandez?" I shrank into
the crowd, hoping that no one would give me away, for the Chinese driver
looked like the devil incarnate. He was "Ming the Merciless" from the
movie serial *Flash Gordon*. Oh, how horribly cruel was that evil man and
this wild truck driver seemed as out of control as the emperor of the Planet
Mongo.

"If I get any more complaints from any of you," the truck driver said,
his red eyes sweeping over the cowed fruit pickers, "this will happen." Like
the blade of a rising guillotine the driver lifted his long knife up and with a
heave of his hand brought it down onto a pineapple resting on the wooden
box. Almost severed from the body, the leaf-filled crown slowly tipped over
the box and fell to the ground. Juice flowed from the clean cut, muddying
the ground where the head of the fruit lay.

I shuddered. For some reason I thought of Marie Antoinette and wondered how she felt when the blade, meant to be used for the decapitation of
bovines, cut her head away from her neck. Dr. Guillotine's device slashed to
death thousands of people during the French Revolution.

After the driver's theatrics, the pineapple pickers melted away, receiving from the *luna* lady their rows to work that day. I watched the arrogant
truck driver leave, red dust flinging from his tires. I made up my mind not
to reveal the morning events to my mother. She worked twenty years for
the cannery and knew the top people. Protecting her young one, she did
not realize what her good intentions produced. In the fields you did not
have your mother's aprons to cling to. You fought your own battles like you
did in the schoolyard when the bully threatened to put stars in your eyes.
Would the driver sever my neck? I didn't think so, but prudence dictated a
low profile rather than bravado.

I proceeded to work, wondering if my complaints to Mom had been ill-
considered. The driver was now an enemy who could do real physical harm,
not like the *kahuna* who preyed on your fear of the supernatural. Working
for big boss pineapple along with his many subjects who sought his favor
for the money that he provided had its real world problems. Do you snitch
on a fellow worker for his misdeeds or remain silent and escape harm?

In a row nearby my Japanese friend, who had disappeared for a time
after Pearl Harbor, wrestled with a large pineapple. Sensing my gaze he
looked up, meeting my eyes. His inscrutable face revealed nothing except

I noted a slight upturning of his lips. Was it a smile or smirk? With this solitary signal he returned to freeing the fruit from its rooting on the parent shrub.

Despite the blazing sun of a hot day, I finished my assigned rows by the lunch time whistle. At the edge of the red dust road bordering the rows of pineapple shrubs, I turned up a box and plopped on its wooden top, spreading out my booted feet to ease the pain from the blisters that had formed on them. For most of my growing years I had run and played shoeless. In this new working environment I could no longer be the barefoot boy with cheeks of tan.

My Japanese friend working nearby came with his tin lunch pail and sat beside me. "Want some *ume?*" he said.

I smiled, relieved that he wished to talk, for his friendship had been missed. "Sure. How about some dried fish?" I said, offering him a dark sliver of sundried salted *akule.*

We exchanged gifts and sat munching our ume and fish that we swallowed amidst gobs of white rice. "What's happened to you?" I said, breaking the short silence between us.

My friend's eyes narrowed, but he remained silent. Had I offended him by my question? Was there a dark secret to be hidden whose revelation would produce a storm of trouble? I did not know, but the morning had taught me that forbearance was wise and prodding statements could produce trouble.

We ate in silence until I offered my friend a cookie.

"You did good," he said.

"What do you mean?"

"Chinese don't like Japanese. Most of the workers in the truck are Japanese."

"You mean the *Pake* driver wanted to hurt us to get even with Japan for fighting China?"

My friend smiled, saying, "Maybe so."

"Why didn't any of you complain?"

"We're ashamed. All of us are suspected traitors. Smartest thing for Japanese is shut your mouth and say nothing bad about anybody."

My friend rose and started toward the row he had been working on. He looked back and said, "Thanks."

That evening I asked my Aunt Maggie about this strange conversation and why my friend was "ashamed."

"The war is hard on the Japanese in Hawai'i. Too many old people refused to give up their ties with Japan. They registered Hawai'i-born babies with their home village, making them citizens of two countries. They made them speak Japanese, honor their ancestors, and the emperor."

"So when the war came what the old people did hurt their children."

"Yes. You know what happened to Yutaka. He gave up his chance to be elected because of the trouble it would cause. Good thing he did or we might all be in jail on Sand Island."

"But why is my friend ashamed?"

"Have you seen his father since the war started?"

"No."

"Maybe he is an alien who was taken away by the military. I don't know, but Japanese families suspected of disloyalty have great shame. For them the sensible thing to do is to remain quiet."

"But how do we make it better for my friend and Yutaka?"

My aunt sighed, saying, "I don't know. But Japanese boys are desperate to prove their loyalty. Thousands are signing up to go to war against the Germans. Maybe it will make a difference."

Blisters ached my feet, reminding me of the new knowledge I had gained from this eventful day. Somehow, the war was pushing me out of my carefree apathetic island life into a new world where shoes, clean clothes, and speaking proper English were required.

CHAPTER 31

Opportunities For Success

War with its devastation brought Hawaiians opportunities for the achievement of financial well-being. Prior to Pearl Harbor, native people had little chance to succeed. The economy was agricultural with sugar and pineapple as its kingpins. The plantations and canneries controlled the economic life of the islands and those of brown color did not make it into the top level of the Big Five businesses.

I am not implying that the Hawaiians of my family gained success by means of wartime profiteering, or the black market, or some form of illicit acts like prostitution. What I am saying is that success came legitimately from the influx of hundreds of thousands of American soldiers and civilians brought to Hawai'i to fight the war.

The thousand-seat theater that had been dubbed "Fernandez's Folly" before Pearl Harbor became an entertainment Mecca of Kaua'i following the Japanese attack. Forty thousand soldiers would transition in and out of the Garden Island as they went through jungle training and amphibious warfare exercises in preparation for battle in the Pacific.

The Roxy became the focal point of relaxation for soldiers on Kaua'i. Because of this my part-Hawaiian parents could pay off their debts and find financial success after years of penury and failure. There were other Hawaiian success stories.

One evening my mother said, "Pack your brown suitcase. We are going to Honolulu."

"Why?" I protested.

"To see Chinese herb doctor for your asthma and visit with Uncle Joe."

Early in the morning, we headed for Barking Sands, the only airport on the island. It was an arduous, boring, two-hour car ride to the far west end of Kaua'i. The DC 3 was dark inside. All the windows were blacked out. "Wartime precautions," a stewardess said.

I wondered how the pilots knew where to fly if they were also blacked out. But we took off okay and after an hour, landed.

It was my first time in the big city of Honolulu and it seemed like a town of bedlam and chaos. Aircraft engines roared and dozens of autos filled the streets with honking and chugging engines. There were signal lights and tall buildings that Kaua'i didn't have.

Uncle Joe met us at the airport. He was a short man with a paunch that signaled a love of eating. His open-armed undershirt revealed a shock of white hair on his chest, matching the unruly mat upon his head. Between his lips was clamped the stub of a cigar, the grey ashes of which fell like snow onto his chest.

"Come with me," he rasped in a hoarse voice while keeping the cigar held firmly between his teeth.

I was amazed that he could talk, walk, and smoke all at the same time.

We motored along Ala Moana Boulevard and eventually entered downtown Honolulu. In all my life, I had never seen so many Chinese people thronging the streets.

"This is Chinatown," Uncle Joe announced, "and here is my store."

Inside the large shop were displays of beads, necklaces, straw hats, mats, curios, and all kinds of Pacific Island junk. There were throngs of military personnel and civilians looking and buying.

"Sister, I wanted to show you what I'm doing. There is lots of money to be made in selling to the *haoles*. I'm renting a second store. Need to fill it with island stuff. The family can make it for me on Kaua'i."

My mom began speaking in Hawaiian. It was a language I had never been taught. Why? Because the family was ashamed to admit they had Hawaiian blood. But when the elders wanted to talk serious business, they spoke in the native tongue.

I tried my best to tune in on the conversation, but could only catch a few words. It appeared that Uncle Joe had tried several schemes during the course of his life, each one costing the family more than they could afford. But this time he looked like he had a winner with a business that could only get better as more and more military poured into the island.

Finally they came to an understanding and I was whisked off to a Chinese apothecary. "My boy has asthma," Mom said to the herbalist who looked like Fu Manchu.

The druggist reached into jars, pulling out all kinds of vile looking, evil smelling, herbs and petrified leaves. He gave Mom several packages.

"Boil this in water," the man said, holding a horribly smelling bundle in his hand. "Drink all of it. Every day boil another package."

There was such a horrid smell rising from the herbs, I gagged and barely kept the vomit down. Uncle Joe puffed heavily on his cigar. I finally understood why stogie smoking is necessary. It masks unwelcome smells with the pungent aroma of tobacco.

My ordeal was not over. When we got to Uncle's home, Mom pulled out a pot, filled it with water, and boiled a packet of Chinese herbs. The kitchen filled with the smell of decayed leaves and who knows what other loathsome things mixed into the brew. The concoction cooked oily black and appeared to be Satan's blood.

My mind whirled back to Hanalei beach when I was young. An anemic *haole* boy, his skin white as the clouds above, dug in the sand building a castle. I joined his efforts and in an eerie voice he said the words of the three witches, "Fire burn, cauldron bubble, in the cauldron boil and bake, eye of newt and toe of frog, wool of bat and tongue of dog." I have never forgotten that moment, for the boy treated me as inferior for not knowing Shakespeare. His mother, on noticing me, banned me from playing with her son.

"Can't we put sugar in it?" I begged as I looked at the loathsome brew, remembering the ingredients that had gone into the "hell-broth" of the witches' stew. My protests were ignored. I was ordered to drink the whole mess, however difficult its swallowing might be. Oh, what ugly dreams came that night as the unsettling liquid transitioned me from snake, to blind worm, then frog.

At dawn, I examined every part of my body to be sure that I had not turned into an evil critter. Mother said at breakfast, "Uncle Joe and I will be gone all day. Play in the house. Cook the herbs and drink them."

This last command was like a death sentence. I knew the dreaded brew would make me sick. After they left I decided to explore Honolulu. Yesterday, we had driven past River Street. In a seedy section of town a theater advertised *Ecstasy*. Scores of men in khaki stood in line. Not far away, another movie house advertised an Abbott and Costello show. I hopped on a bus and headed for the theaters.

At Aala Park I found a Mecca of honky-tonk entertainment. Beer bars, saloons, fun games, and lines of soldiers, sailors, and marines waiting to do something. I snuck up to the movie theater advertising *Ecstasy*, not knowing what I had stumbled onto. A picture poster displayed a nude young lady running through a forest. The caption billed Hedy Lamarr as "the most beautiful woman in the world." Other posters claimed there were "sex scenes" in the movie. Wow! This was a must-see show. But I quickly found out that only adult males were allowed in.

I had seen drakes and roosters mounting female birds, and I left the theater disappointed that I could not witness ecstasy between a man and woman. The word itself made me believe that the act of love was something grand.

I strolled into the park intending to head into downtown Honolulu. A couple of boys threw a ball back and forth and I stood to watch, carefully avoiding eye contact which could lead to trouble. A loose ball came in my direction and I threw it back. Soon I became part of the game. The guys were really good kids and we began talking. I told them that I had wanted to see the movie *Ecstasy*.

"You like see da kine?"

I nodded my head.

"Come, we go see."

I followed them to River Street which winds along Nuuanu Stream. Within a short walk, I saw a long line of servicemen waiting by some cottage buildings. "What's this?" I said.

"Guys waiting to get into a 'bull pen,'" said one of my new friends. "Want to go see?"

My courage rapidly evaporated. What would I tell my mom? What about the Catholic priests and nuns who taught me that sex is evil, only permitted in marriage, and only allowed to create children? I visualized that I would have to confess to mortal sin and say endless "Our Fathers" and "Hail Marys."

"No thanks," I said, and scooted off into downtown Honolulu to see an Abbott and Costello movie.

A story of prostitution would be written several months later called *Honolulu Harlot*. An angry whore detailed the scores of houses of sin that existed in Honolulu with the connivance of the U.S. military and the police. The purpose of these whore houses was to keep the morale of the soldier boys high before they went into battle.

* * *

We returned to Kaua'i. Mother galvanized the family into doing Uncle Joe's bidding. Into the forests I went to gather koa seeds and dry hala leaves. The hala plant is ugly. Its roots rise above the ground like a witch's broomstick, its long trunk topped by an unruly mop of green leaves. These are like droopy sword blades bordered with thorns on the edges. When dry, they are exceedingly tough and used to weave mats, hats, fans, and bowls. It is one of the few native plants that the first settlers found when they came to Hawai'i. The fruit of the plant is so hard that it can only be eaten after extensive cooking. It served as a starvation food for the early colonizers when there was nothing else to eat.

The extended family available to fulfill Uncle Joe's contract for goods amounted to a dozen people. For days an assembly line of adults and children strung koa seed leis and made hala products. Aunt Katie was an expert at making feather leis and the sea shells I gathered Mother made into leis or interesting gifts.

Uncle Joe came to Kaua'i to survey our efforts. Puffing on his cigar he pronounced the work satisfactory but not perfect. He demanded more output and quality, saying, "Can't sell what the kids make. Let them gather and sisters you make."

He disgusted me. Multiple cuts ached, caused by stripping away the thorns of hala leaves. My fingers had numerous needle pokes from stringing together boiled soft koa seeds. I thought what I had created was worthy to be bought, but my uncle did not think so. However, that was our family for you, short on praise and long on criticism. I guess the idea was to force you to do better through disapproval.

What we constructed was packaged and sent to Honolulu. Wartime shipping had eased since Japanese submarines no longer prowled island waters. We were winning in the Pacific.

Whether our efforts made Uncle Joe's fortune, I do not know. But he sold his two curio stores in downtown Honolulu for enough money to live comfortably for the rest of his life. He left for San Francisco, failing to reward any of the island family and failing to help my aunt and her four children stranded on the mainland by an errant husband.

Uncle Joe kept his fortune in a well-packed money belt around his waist. His undoing came because of his love for loose women and a fast life. Inducing a prostitute into his San Francisco hotel room, she let in her pimp who beat him up and stole his money.

Despite losing all he had, Joe was like the cat with nine lives. He met a rich lonely woman in the City by the Bay, wooed, won, and traveled with her back to Hawai'i. She became his wife. I really don't know how many marriages my uncle had. He was a charmer of women despite his stogie, pot belly, and white undershirt that failed to conceal his hairy chest.

Japan's attack had moved the island's economy away from its total dependence on agriculture. No longer were Hawaiians confined to the scanty earnings of hula maids, surf riders, musicians, laborers, and servants. Catering to the wartime needs of the thousands of soldiers and civilians who came to the islands, fortunes were made by Hawaiians. This new wealth was not acquired by illicit activities, but through hard work and ingenuity. It would be the earnings of the Roxy that would give my sister and me the opportunity to become educated and achieve what had been unattainable for my parents, escape from poverty.

Bertolt Brecht's play, *Mother Courage*, tells the story of an old woman who profits from war. Her pursuit of wealth by catering to soldiers ends in tragedy as her three children were killed in combat. War is not an event that any sane person would want. Death and tragedy are the consequences of this ultimate human insanity. But war creates changes in an economy which gives those who are at the bottom of the money pyramid the opportunity to rise up and secure financial well-being. War also causes political and social changes that could not occur without it.

CHAPTER 32

The Winds Of Change

Before the war, the plantations had criticized the predominantly Japanese population of Hawai'i as stooges for the emperor, intent on seizing the islands for Japan. After the Pearl Harbor attack, this apparent hostility of the Big Five companies threatened the Issei and Nissei population with internment on the U.S. mainland.

Cooler heads prevailed, for it became obvious to the military that Oahu could not be America's Pacific Bastion if one hundred thousand Japanese were shipped to the United States. But hostility to the Japanese population in the islands was strong during the early years of combat in the Pacific. Unions were suppressed, labor leaders jailed as agitators, and Japanese politicians shamed into surrendering their offices.

Nissei begged to prove their loyalty to America and some four thousand Hawaii boys and twelve hundred mainland internees were formed into a regimental combat team to fight the Nazis in Europe. Reports by the news media in the Mediterranean described the insane courage and tenacity of these men. Correspondent Ernie Pyle said, "In the face of great odds where others would give up (the Japanese boys) keep fighting." The Associated Press said, "The courage of the Japanese boys (is) beyond the call of duty."

Our family was a reflection of the "melting pot of the Pacific" composed of the many races that had come to work in the sugar fields and after their indenture ended, intermarried and built the racially-blended kaleidoscope of Hawai'i.

Because of the combat exploits of a few brave men, the attitude toward the Japanese throughout the islands moved from hostility to praise. It had not been an easy transition for our Nissei into this new acceptability. They had been vilified as traitors and placed in the same category as the Norwegian Fifth Columnists. But despite the outrageous treatment by American citizens, they remained loyal to our country and gave up sons in the fight against Fascism.

Since the allies were winning on all fronts, I asked my Aunt Maggie, "What will happen after the war is over? Do we go back to the way it was before?"

My aunt, who was the image of her mother Julia with a saucer-round face and piggish nose, looked at me with owl-shaped brown eyes. "William, the days of the plantation system are over."

"You mean no more labor camps and company stores?"

"I think so."

"What about Yutaka, will he run again? My dad says the Republicans are strong."

My aunt shook her head. "Yutaka won't try again. But when the war is over and the Japanese boys return home, watch out."

I tired of this conversation and went off to play. These were matters beyond my understanding. I did notice that my Japanese friends were more visible now and made more noise. Obedience to parents was more relaxed. I noticed the older folks grappling with the new independence of their children. In the past, it had been unheard of for a good Japanese girl to go out with a *haole,* especially a soldier. But now they were doing so. Letters from the fighting men reported on their amours with American or European girls. Often they begged forgiveness for breaking with tradition.

Picking pineapples in the summer of 1944, I thought over the change that had come to our lives because of the war. Before Pearl Harbor, I was raised in ancient beliefs of the *kahuna* controlling my life through occult powers. But the war had proved that evil words and prayers were nothing but superstitious mumbo jumbo.

We had been raised to believe that only the *haole* could achieve wealth, for they were smarter. But my father, uncle, and several Chinese and Japanese that I knew had accumulated money because of the war.

Still, there seemed to be an invisible barrier to my escaping the life of a laborer in the fields. I recalled the derisive laughter of the young white kid when I said, "Who's Shakespeare?" Then there were the slights when I was told, "Hawaiians sit in the rear." Even my dad was upset at my dark skin saying, "You are as black as the ace of spades."

Breaking the yellow fruits and hurling them into my sack, I thought myself doomed because I am a brown Hawaiian and would always be held back. What chance did I have in a world ruled by the Caucasian? Should I stay out of the sun and let my half-white blood change my skin to tan? That was not practical. Living in Hawai'i, I could not escape the sunshine. Besides, I was not ashamed to be Hawaiian like the older members of my family.

They could not be blamed for feeling as they did. They grew up at a time when the Hawaiian monarchy was overthrown by white business-men, the deposed Hawaiian Queen vilified as a black savage and the few Hawaiians still alive labeled lazy and ignorant.

Sweating under the broad brim of my straw hat, I studied the mountain above me, the tops of its green slimed stone, jagged like a saw blade. Cascading waterfalls over the eons had cleaved the rock into numerous indentations and I could see that the hole in Anahola Mountain was getting larger as erosion crumbled its rock sides.

It seemed that the natural order of things is change. The volcano that built the island had stopped erupting. Its massive conical caldera eroded over time by winds and rain. Scientists said that one day Kaua'i would be nothing more than a large pancake-shaped atoll in the sea. Could I metamorphose into something else? Could I escape this trap I am in and change? More important, did I want to? Life is easy, simple, and stress-free in the tropics. I learned from my experience with the truck driver that there were negative reactions when you pushed against the accepted order of things. Life can be simpler if you did not make waves.

Covered with red dust, I returned home to clean up. I was in for a shock. My mother said, "Your father is leaving for San Francisco to retire there."

"What about you?"

"I will go later, after you get into Kamehameha Schools."

In the late spring, Doctor Bailey, principal of a school in Honolulu, had interviewed me. "A Hawaiian princess willed her land into trust to create two schools for Hawaiian children," he said.

"Only kids with Hawaiian blood can go there?" I asked.

"Yes," he answered.

Remembering the talk I had with the kindly bespectacled, bald-headed administrator of the school, I said, "Mom, I haven't been accepted."

"Well you can stay with your Aunt Katie until you are."

"You're going to leave me again like you did the last time."

"Your father is making me go."

"Colleen is going too, like she did before."

"Yes, she will be heading off to college."

It was a devastating announcement. It meant that I would live again with relatives, subject to whatever whims or demands they would make.

"Who is going to run the Roxy?" I asked.

"Your Cousin Alice. When you grow up and finish college, your father wants you to manage the theater."

Her words shattered my world. I had hated being given to the Morgan family to be cared for when Dad and Mom went to the mainland in the 1930s to study movie theaters. The older brother in the family was a tough, mean taskmaster and ruled with an iron hand. At least he no longer lived with my aunt since he married and established his own home. But the scars of that experience were deep in my psyche. I had no objection to remaining at Kapa'a School, but could it be a springboard to a better life?

I pondered these issues as fall came and the time for my mother's departure was imminent. Acceptance had not arrived from Kamehameha Schools and my eighth grade year began. A few days after the start of the semester, I received a summons to the principal's office.

My Aunt Maggie was there. She taught at Kapa'a School. "You are going home. Get ready to go to Honolulu."

"What?"

"A Waimea boy decided not to go to Kamehameha. You are next on the list."

My mother waited outside and drove home. She was excited. "Everything has worked out. I can leave for the mainland knowing you're in a good school."

She helped me pack my brown suitcase. We ate supper and I wondered whether I would ever see her again. She kept saying, "Your father is forcing me to go."

We woke early and took the long drive to Barking Sands airport. Traveling past luxuriant green fields of sugar cane that stretched from the mountains to the sea, I wondered if life as I knew it was changing. It seemed impossible to happen. Sugar had been king since my birth.

At the airport the radial engine of the DC 3 roared with power, propelling the aircraft along the tarmac heading into a blue sky. I sensed that this departure from Kaua'i and my island friends signified something enormous. I was off to a school for Hawaiian children where my family had been promised I would receive a first rate education. I was leaving a tiny plantation- controlled island for a big city with all of its exciting facets that piqued my interest on the visit with Uncle Joe months ago.

Would this Hawaiian school be a stepping stone for change in my life? Would it be the means of escaping the hard work of a pineapple picker? My cousin Alice had admonished me before I left home to study hard and make it to college. Many Hawaiian boys had failed to do so. I decided to try.

Amazon Review: 5 STARS:

"This book is truly a delight. If you've ever watched an eight year old boy getting himself into trouble and wondered, "What could he possibly be thinking?" this book will provide insight. Growing up on The Garden Island as told through the eyes of a young boy will have you alternately laughing and crying. Bill Fernandez recounts stories of fishing, friendships, having little but sharing all, and the quest to find Santa Claus...a wonderful mixture of island history coupled with personal experience and an extended family... describes the importance of the ocean to Hawaiian culture, the ways the bombing of Pearl Harbor severely altered island life, bringing GIs, bomb shelters, curfews, rationing and the threat of Japanese American internment to the paradise of Kaua'i." (Reviewer: June, May, 2013)

About the Author

Bill Fernandez is a retired judge of Native Hawaiian descent who grew up barefoot running on the Kaua'i reefs in a much simpler time. He graduated from Kamehameha High School and Stanford University with B.A. and J.D. degrees. After retiring from his legal career in Santa Clara County, CA, Bill returned to the Kaua'i home his mother bought with her pineapple cannery earnings and turned to writing. *Rainbows Over Kapa'a* describes the family movie theater and how Kapa'a grew out of marshland. He also gives Hawaiian history talks along with his wife, Judith, who created PowerPoint slide shows for them. Bill was recently appointed by the governor to the Juvenile Justice State Advisory Council.

Few people have lived under military occupation in the United States. Bill did. It changed his life.

Bill Fernandez: Talk Story

By Bill Buley/The Garden Island Newspaper/Kaua'i   May 12, 2013

Growing up in Kapa'a, Bill Fernandez wanted to be a fisherman. He tells stories of free diving, spearing fish and leaving a trail of blood in the water. And that, of course, attracted predators. "The reef shark will come, and sometimes, you get one of these tigers. Those guys are vicious," he said. "Fortunately, I'm still here. After that shark makes some passes by you, you do get a little concerned. Get out of the water as fast as you can." Fernandez laughs and smiles as he continues sharing his memories. "The rule of thumb is, don't feed them. Once they get fed, they're pretty hard to stop." He never feared the water.

As a boy during World War II, he delivered cigarettes to machine gun nests not far from his home. He shined shoes. He rolled dice. He survived. "I like to say when I was born, I had one foot in Christianity, and one foot in the old Kahuna system. My mother was raised in the old Hawaiian way. She still believed in those things, although we went to church every Sunday." His goal, up to his 18th birthday, was to fish the water off Kaua'i and eventually retire. Well, the retirement part worked out. Career-wise, not so much. Fernandez did more than perhaps even he imagined. "Times change," he said. "You get motivated." Absolutely.

Consider these accomplishments of Bill Fernandez: • Graduate of Kamehameha Schools in Honolulu • Graduate of Stanford University and Law School • Attorney for 15 years in California • Served as a judge in the California Superior Court • Mayor of Sunnyvale, Calif. • Author of *Kaua'i Kids in Peace and War* and *Rainbows Over Kapa'a*.

Retired today, Fernandez and his wife Judith live in the same oceanfront home his mother Agnes bought around 1927 with her pineapple earnings, a beautiful green house with white trim, and a front porch perfect for entertaining guests or enjoying the view. "My mother worked in the cannery at the time, 25 cents a day. She bought this house," he said. "Since, that home has withstood four tidal waves and four or five hurricanes," Fernandez said. "You know the worst thing that ever happened to this house? You see the glass table? It was turned over in 'Iniki'. That's the only thing that's ever happened to it." "And the glass wasn't even cracked," Judith added.

"During those storms, debris filled their yard, homes were destroyed, roads disappeared. Yet the Fernandez home stood strong. "This house has survived all of those disasters, where everything else has fallen down," he said. Fernandez paused when asked how it survived. "It's got the protection of the Kahuna," he said. "Somehow it got blessed well, or it's on sacred ground. Because everything else you see around you is new." "Agnes is protecting us," Judith added. "That's why we call this place Agnes' house."

Fernandez has indeed led what some might call a charmed life, but it's not about charm. It's about hard work, about overcoming obstacles such as asthma, setting goals, self belief, and a dream to be part of the world. He wants to encourage others to explore the world, to push beyond their limits, to believe they can achieve their dreams. It's part of why he wrote those books about growing up on Kaua'i, a time when some 25,000 people lived here, and how he found his way to Menlo Park, Calif., where he owns a home, and to Sunnyvale, Calif., where he was mayor and helped create a masterplan.

"I wrote *Rainbows Over Kapa'a* because of my father and mother, poor Hawaiians, how they struggled to finally make it. There's a lot of background history in it. I wanted to tell about those folks and their hard times. *Kaua'i Kids in Peace and War* describes growing up on an isolated island, about believing there was more beyond us and I wanted to find it."

Q: What was it like growing up here?

"It was a real time of innocence on an isolated island. You don't know anything about the outside world, a fantasy land, where you can't believe there's anything else. You also have to make anything you want. When the boat comes in it isn't bringing stuff for kids. They're bringing something for plantation or canneries or the mom and pop businesses. You have to do a lot of hand work and get people to help. To make a canoe, you get an old piece of corrugated metal, bend it, shape it, and go out into this ocean in your little tin canoe and struggle in the sea.

"There was always the struggle with the ocean. This powerful thing scared you, but it's delightful. There are so many interesting mysteries under that water. I loved spearfishing. You always found new little treasures, a piece of coral or a forest of black coral, a whole new fantasy land.

"The problem growing up on a small island, you hadn't any broad vision. You didn't see a bigger picture. Ambition was not part of your life. Plantations controlled us. The whole island was like a barony of the rich. All the little peons like myself and others were regulated by the plantation."

Q: What motivated you to achieve so much?

"There has to be a better life. War World II starts, Pearl Harbor. You suddenly have thousands of soldiers from the Mainland descend upon you. You become aware of history, that Hitler's going through Europe and causing trouble. These guys coming here to train to fight have been living interesting lives. You suddenly realize there is a bigger world than this little cubicle. You become curious, you want to know. You want to learn. You want to become educated. "That's why I went to Kamehameha Schools, to learn about the bigger picture. As my teacher said on my graduation, "You came here like a country bumpkin, and you're going out as a leader."

Q: You're named after your father. What was his influence?

"My father always said, because he had only a third-grade education he really felt that if he understood the law, he would have been much more successful than he was. He had a lot of different businesses that turned out to be failures.

"In 1939 he built the biggest movie theater in all the islands, 1,050 seat Roxy. Everybody said that's a folly, that's foolish, and really it was. Come 1941, he can't pay the bills, his mortgage, the bank is foreclosing. Guess what? Pearl Harbor happens. Martial law is imposed. All civil proceedings stop, so the foreclosure can't proceed, and now descending on the island is the Rainbow Division out of New York. Twenty-five thousand men here for training. Where are they going to go for entertainment? The movies! I still remember Christmas Eve, my dad is talking to my mother in the kitchen, he said, "We have paid the $50,000 mortgage and we have $50,000 in the bank." That's why I called the story *Rainbows over Kapa'a,* because, like the Chinese before him who planted rice in the mud of Kapa'a and made their fortune, he got his pot of gold by building the Roxy theater like he did."

Q: What do you think of Kaua'i today?

"It's much, much better. I tell you, when I was growing up, you lived the plantation life. There were rules and regulations that you had to follow, unwritten laws that you obeyed. They were a community of elite and of course, we were the dregs. Among the ethnic groups that worked on the plantations, there was camaraderie. You were friendly. But there was class separation between the elite and the rest of us.

"The great thing that happened after the war, the sons of the plantation workers got educated with the GI Bill. They realized that there's a bigger world out there, democracy, that all men are created equal, and they began to make change after the war. In '46 you had the great strike of the plantation and cannery workers. When it was over, agricultural workers in Hawai'i were the highest paid in the world, $1.21 an hour, not much, but it shows the disparity. You have a greater sense of equality now than ever before. That's the wonder of what's happened."

Q: Looking back on your career, is there anything you consider your greatest accomplishment?

"Well, as a judge one of the most interesting cases that I had was a Down syndrome child that the parents wanted to allow to die. He needed a life-saving operation for his heart or he would slowly suffocate. The case had been tried in juvenile court because of the need for surgery. It made national headlines. A year and a half later the case shows up in my court, where surrogate parents were requesting guardianship of this young boy. After a two-week trial, I found a way, creating some new law called 'in the best interest of the child'. I found that these surrogate parents could be guardians of this child. He survived the surgery. So in terms of the law, that was one of the high-point cases.

"In terms of lifetime achievement, I feel I had a big part in creating Sunnyvale, and making it the great city that it is today. When I was on the City Council, we had a bond issue to build fire stations, parks, streets, underground sewer and water, a number of civic projects. We needed a two-thirds majority to pass it. I feel very happy I was able to be part of getting it done. It really made the city what it is today. That's an achievement I'm very proud of. I wanted to come back here and do something that would be a great help to our community, because I think Kaua'i is a great place."

Q: Was there a person who most influenced you?

"One of my Kamehameha teachers opened my eyes to not only new ways of thinking, but also that you can achieve. In my time, there was a feeling of real despair among Hawaiian boys, that they could not do any better than maybe working in a hotel or being a gas station operator or working for the telephone company, they couldn't go any further. He really thought that I could do better. So it's the mentoring. I've talked to many people who are successful, and you've always got to have a mentor somewhere early on in your career, or when you're growing up, to move you forward."

Q: How about overcoming asthma in your childhood? What inspired you?

"Glenn Cunningham. He was a runner in the '30s who almost broke the four-minute mile. He was in a school fire, his brother was killed, and his legs were badly burned. Doctors wanted to amputate. He refused. 'You're not taking my legs.' That's a story that always inspired me, how he was able to develop his legs back to health and be the runner that Roger Bannister eventually became. Glenn was thought to be the first American who might break the four-minute mile. A great story which inspired me because asthma just debilitated me. I was able to force myself to overcome it. This ocean was my doctor."

Q: What would you say to people to encourage them to read your books?

"*Rainbows Over Kapa'a* tells you about the struggle of the poor Hawaiians to try and make it. My father goes after the dream of a large movie theater. *Kaua'i Kids in Peace and War* tells the story of a kid with no ambition, no knowledge of the world, and finally tries to find a way to make a better life. Both are stories of struggles to try and be better, to succeed. Somehow, I made it. 'But for the grace of God'. I used to say that in court a lot. You see this guy that's going to be sentenced to death or prison for 40 years or whatever, and I'd say to myself: 'But for the grace of God go I. I could have been that same kid.'"

Edited for brevity by Judith Fernandez